Beer is for Everyone!
(of Drinking Age)

Em Sauter

ISBN 13: 978-1944937355

Cover design by: Keeli McCarthy

One Peace Books
43-32 22nd Street #204
Long Island City, NY 11101 USA
http://www.onepeacebooks.com

Printed in China
1234546789

Beer is for Everyone!

Of Drinking Age

EM SAUTER

To Samuel Adams White Ale circa
2006, the brew that made me fall
for beer, hard. This is your fault.

CONTENTS

Beers and what goes into them!

Foreword

THE ABILITY TO TASTE and review beer goes well beyond simply identifying flavors. It's a skill that comes with time, commitment, education, and getting outside of your preferred flavor wheelhouse.

You also have to like to drink. A lot.

For those of us inclined towards making the fermented beverage a bigger part of our daily experience this is a wonderful time to be alive. There's a global renaissance happening that is reviving long-forgotten styles, creating new flavor combinations, embracing technology, promoting agriculture, and most importantly bringing people together.

Beer has been in the background of the human experience for a millennium, from achievements in art and science, and the planning, birth, and fall of empires, to everyday experiences like happy hours and backyard barbeques. Throughout all this, beer was rarely the center of conversation.

Today, as we close in on 6,000 breweries in the United States and scores more around the world, there are countless conversations happening — right now — about specific beers, breweries, hop flavors, and more. To make the most of these conversations, and to show your friends how smart you are, you need to consult the experts first.

Congratulations! The book you're holding will give you the knowledge you need to order and converse with confidence. The talented artist behind this book, Em Sauter, has been on a professional beer journey that's seen her around the world, behind bars, inside breweries, and never far from her next glass and pencils.

I've had the good fortune of knowing Em for many years and hoisting many pints over countless nights. What always strikes me is that she greets every beer like a friend, even the ones she's had many times before or winds up not liking very much. There's an infectious excitement that comes with each new sample that hits the table, but where some of us — too many of us turn to the analytical — she goes for the whimsical.

"This beer smells like a kindly old man," she announced one evening in my dining room during a blind panel for All About Beer Magazine. For everyone else at the table it was immediately clear just what she meant about this pleasant, if not worn, brown ale.

Reviewing beer is hard work. It really is! It takes a strong focus (something that slips after several rounds) and the ability to reset your brain to zero with each new sample, so as to give each a fair shot at glory.

Where some review books might fall into the predictable language of "hoppy" or "malty," this book does not. If beer is for everyone (indeed) than the descriptions should understandable to us all. Specific, not generic.

That's why the reviews you're about to read just work. With a distinct voice and excellent palate, Em draws us into each beer with wide-eyed expectation. She doesn't play favorites and doesn't pull punches, These reviews give a complete picture and go beyond taste - into place.

Before I met Em, I was a fan of her work. Beer is a visual experience with color, head, and carbonation playing important roles in how we perceive taste and aroma. Ask just about anyone and they'll tell you that certain beers taste better based on where you're drinking it. For many brewers, where they make beer is almost as important as what they put into it.

Thanks to the nature of her visual reviews, Em takes us to where each beer tastes best. She gives us a sense of location, and her colorful imagery brings a new depth to what could otherwise be a dull experience.

That's what sets this book apart. It's why you picked it up in the first place and exactly why you should get a beer, sit down,

and immerse yourself in this wonderful world – created by not only an expert but, like you, a fan.

Cheers,
John Holl

Author, *American Craft Beer Cookbook*
Senior Editor, *Craft Beer and Brewing Magazine*

Beer is for...

That's a bold claim, but I stand by it!

It's a shapeshifter- constantly changing

Beer can taste like...

chocolate

wine

basement?!

With brews being from .05 to over 40% ABV

tires?!

whiskey

salad?!

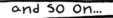

and so on...

Everyone!

Beer is amazingly accessible

Em, can you pick up a six pack from the gas station, or from the new beer shop?

Either place is cool!

Cool

Beer is also amazingly diverse!

It's so much more than that

watery stuff you drank in college

This book is about exploring all facets of beer

And many are easily found at your local store!

Once you find the brew for you...

...you'll want to try more

That's the truth!

Why don't we start with how the world's favorite beverage came to be?

Learnin'

Beer History

The history of brewing dates back thousands of years...

WHOA!

BIG book of stuff

Many historians believe beer got its start in Iraq, by the Sumerians

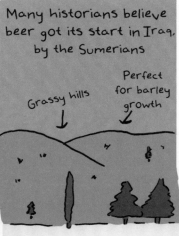

Grassy hills

Perfect for barley growth

By 3000, BC beer making was well-established

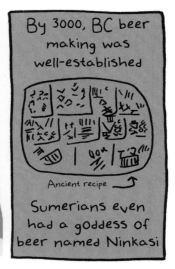

Ancient recipe →

Sumerians even had a goddess of beer named Ninkasi

Egyptians loved beer (hekt) and drank it through straws as a filtration device!

Throughout much of history brewing was done by women!

Egyptian   German   Mayan

Since water was unsafe to drink, even children imbibed

Men took over brewing once it became industrialized

Millions of barrels were produced in Britain alone in the 18th century

Refrigeration changed the game as mass-produced lagers became the norm

In America, prohibition killed a once vibrant industry

NOOOOO!
After the repeal in 1933, less than 100 breweries remained

But in the 70's - Homebrewing became legal again
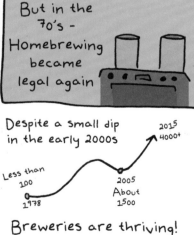
Despite a small dip in the early 2000s

Less than 100
1978
2005 About 1500
2015 4000+

Breweries are thriving!

What does the future hold for beer?
Who knows!?

MARS BREW

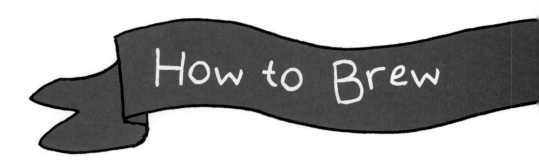

How to Brew

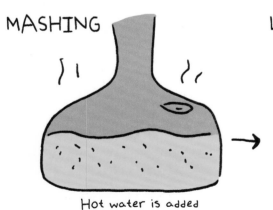

So how does beer get from grain to glass?

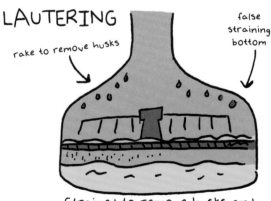

GRAIN SILO

GRIST MILL

Grain is cracked to expose the sugars inside the husks!

MASHING

Hot water is added to the grain

LAUTERING

rake to remove husks

false straining bottom

Strained to remove husks and sprayed with water to get all sugars from the malt

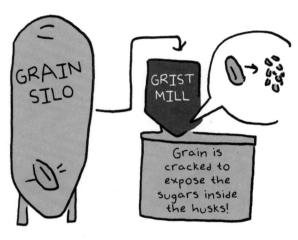

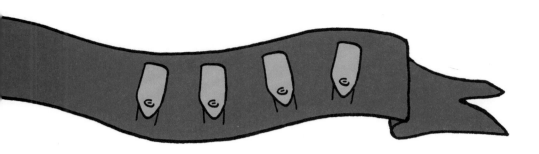

BOIL

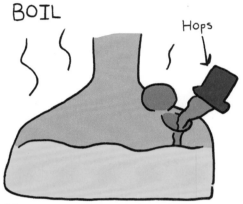

Hops

Hops are added early for flavor or later to add hoppy aroma

WHIRL POOL

Removes hop particulate from the wort (unfermented beer). Then it's chilled to fermentation temp.

FERMENT

Two to five plus weeks depending on style

↓

Temp depends on the style 40 degrees to 90 plus

FILTER/ CONDITION

Conditioning the beer for packaging

plate filter for clarity

PACKAGING

CLING   CLING

ENJOY!

What are

There are over 100 recognized beer styles!

With all those styles

How can you say beer isn't for you?

Beer styles encompass

A whole world of flavor

Pale malts are the base for most beers

Pilsner

Pale

Vienna

Munich

What you do with them creates the style!

Darker malts?

Stouts and porters!

beer styles?

Tons of hops?

Pale Ales and IPAs

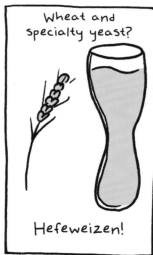

Wheat and specialty yeast?

Hefeweizen!

Not to mention adjuncts!

Adjuncts: ingredients that aren't yeast, hops, water, or malt.

Some popular adjuncts

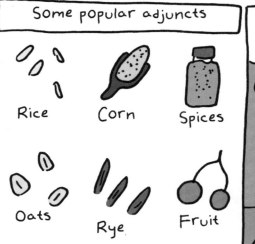

Rice

Corn

Spices

Oats

Rye

Fruit

Beer styles are constantly changing

What is next?!

And the winner for best space yeast beer is...

Brewers Association 100 Years!

HOW TO TASTE BEER

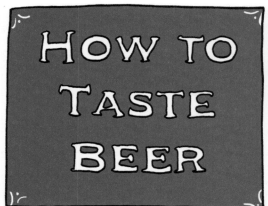

LOOK
Check the color and clarity. Does it have a big head? Is is hazy? Filtered?

SWIRL
Swirling the beer creates the head and activates aroma and taste

SNIFF
Short sniffs are best. What do you smell? No wrong answers!

SIP
Taste the beer. Let the beer wash over your tongue to get a complete experience

THINK!
Did you like it? Not like it? Why? Would you drink it again?

HOW TO BUY BEER

Not all beer shops are created equal

Some treat their beer as a VIP

Things you should look for...

{ Coolers keep beer FRESH! }

More coolers = better quality! (usually)

Beer - especially hoppy beer, is made to drink fresh

Look for date codes on all cans and bottles!

canned 3/4/17

best before 7/19

If stores don't have coolers- make sure the bottles were kept away from light

AHH

you'll skunk me!

And befriend the clerks and owners

They have knowledge!

That IPA you wanted to try came in, Em

PROPER GLASSWARE

Each glass tells the story of the liquid inside...

...And showcases its purpose

From enhancing aromas...

...to simple utility

Since the dawn of time

bronze age malt kiln

From Cyprus

3000 BC

Egyptian

straw to filter

1350 BC

Wooden

900 AD

Pictish Scottish Drinking Horn

From famous carving

1000 AD

Ceramic

1300

Waxed Leather

1700

Silver tankard

1700

Glass

IN DOG YEARS I'VE HAD ONE

Modern

Modern Glassware

STANGE

Stange is German for rod or stick

Small size (6 oz or .2L) means you finish quicker and the beer stays cold

Thin, straight sides

Designed for Altbier or Kölsch

VASE

1^7 oz of .5L in size

Tapered and taller to create a large head of aroma

Narrow base stops heat transfer from hand to beer

Designed for Hefs, Dunkelweizen & Kristalweizen

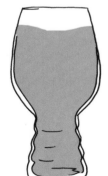

IPA

The newest glass on the shelf

Created for US breweries by German glass blowers

Wide top for head retention, which creates an easy drinking experience

Designed for IPAs and pale ales

CHALICE

Comes in many sizes from tiny to large

Super wide top helps lock in aroma and taste

Heavier than most glassware

Designed for Belgian beers

SNIFTER

Also used for brandy or whiskey

Big bowl made for swirling (which is encouraged)

Brings out the aroma and big flavor of higher ABV beers

Designers for Imperial Stouts, Eisbocks, anything boozy!

TULIP

A glass that holds about 14 oz or .4L

Perfect for beers that function best with bigger head retention

For Belgian styles or higher ABV beers

PILSNER

12 oz or .3L in size

Showcases the sparkling character and color of pilsner style beers while promoting head retention

For lager style beers

STEIN OR MUG

Sturdy, easy to drink out of and comes in various sizes

German steins can also have a top lid which keeps flies/bugs out

Perfect for most German or British styles

NONIC

British "no nick" glasses are easy to stack. Pubs love them!

The bubbles near the top are for grip

Comes in 16 oz and 20 oz sizes

For most British style ales

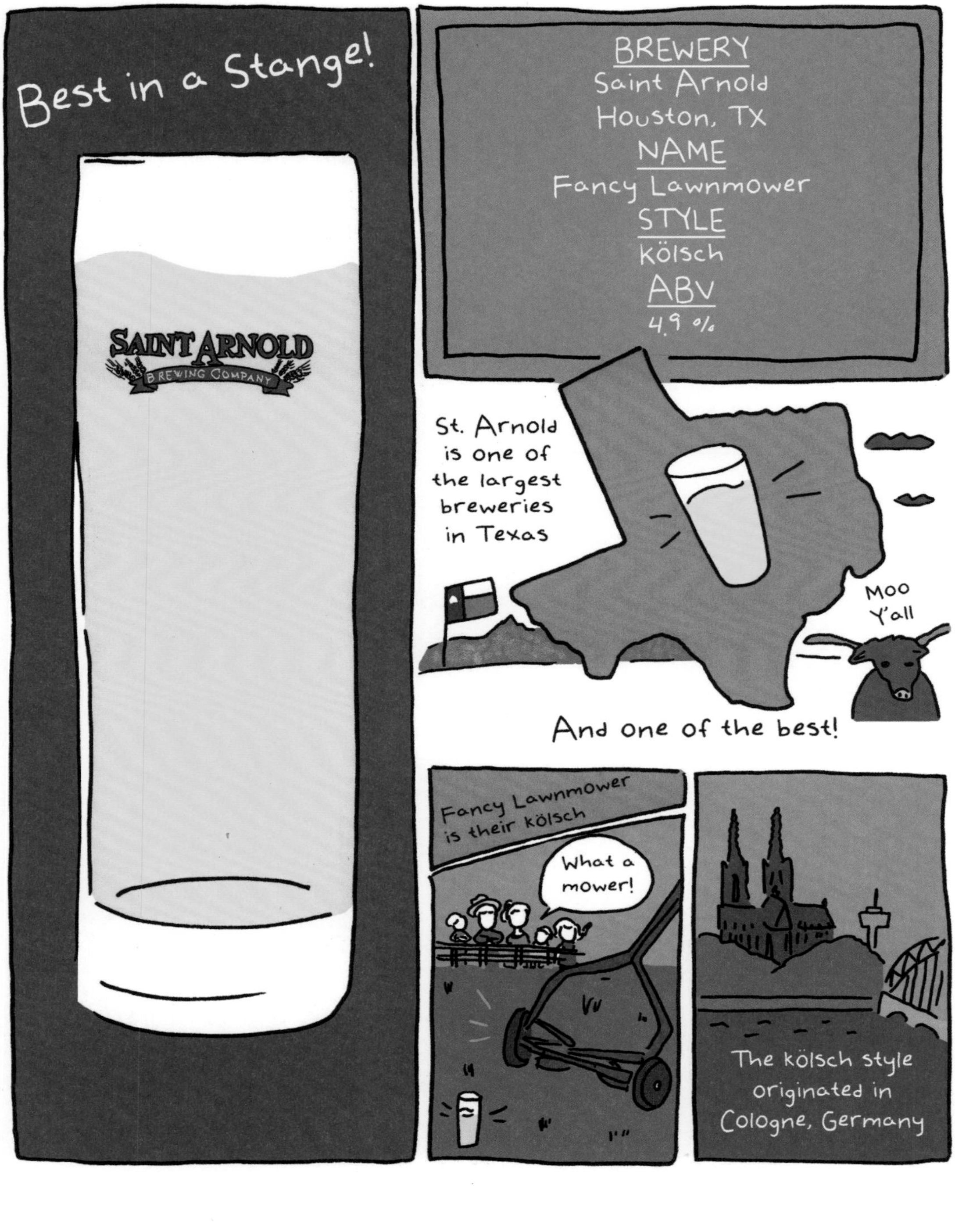
Best in a Stange!
SAINT ARNOLD
BREWING COMPANY
BREWERY
Saint Arnold
Houston, TX
NAME
Fancy Lawnmower
STYLE
kölsch
ABV
4.9 %
St. Arnold is one of the largest breweries in Texas
Moo Y'all
And one of the best!
Fancy Lawnmower is their kölsch
What a mower!
The kölsch style originated in Cologne, Germany

Lawnmower is a term meaning light and sessionable

Perfect for yard work

The name is APT

Truly!

A beer to go toe to toe with the sun

Let's do this

AND WIN!

Kölsch beer is fermented cold like a lager but made with ale yeast so you get a beer that's clean and fruity

Kölsch ales are delicate

And drinkable!

A great Lone Star option for all Texas themed activities

Ropin' Cattle

Line dancin'

Watchin' football

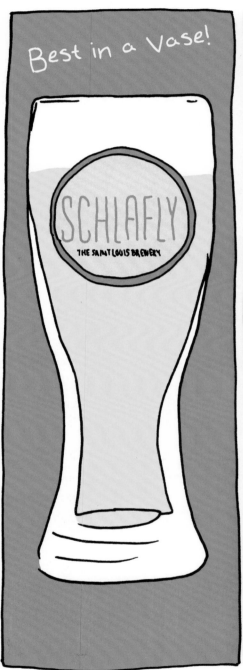

Best in a Vase!

BREWERY
Schlafly
St. Louis, MO
NAME & STYLE
Hefeweizen
ABV
4.4 %

St. Louis
style ribs!

St. Louis has
many tasty
breweries

It's a great
beer town

Schlafly is one of the largest

Say it with me—
SHH-
LAUGH-
FLEE

Their year round hef is very subtle

Good for new drinkers

Aunt Nancy approved!

Oh I like!

Hefs tend to have banana & big clove flavor – but this is toned down

So it makes for a more approachable experience!

What do you think?

It's good!

Now I want to try more beers like this!

Well, I'm sure I can think of a few...

Best in an IPA glass!

Beer'd BREWING CO.

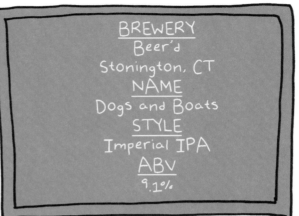

BREWERY
Beer'd
Stonington, CT
NAME
Dogs and Boats
STYLE
Imperial IPA
ABV
9.1%

Beer from my home state!

CT only had a few breweries when I was 21

Now we have over 40

Beer'd makes awesome IPAs

They're brewed right near the shore

Beer'd is owned by a husband and wife

And don't forget Lilly and Tucker!

Their two pooches

Their beers are top notch!

My fav is Dogs & Boats

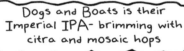

Dogs and Boats is their Imperial IPA- brimming with citra and mosaic hops

Also a nice light malt backbone!

mystic

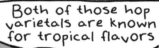

Both of those hop varietals are known for tropical flavors

This beer hides the ABV almost too well

Alcohol? Where are you?

haha

Perfect for a sunset cruise with your best pal...

...Or at many fine CT restaurants and bars...

Connecticut: Not just a state you drive through to get to better states!

Best in a Pilsner Glass!

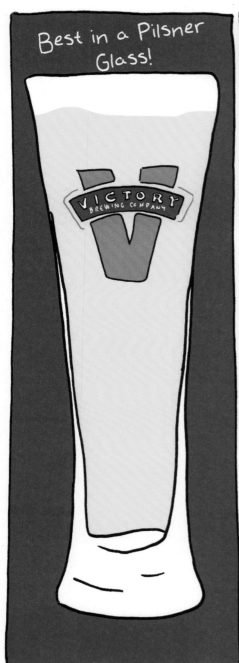

BREWERY
Victory
Downingtown, PA
NAME
Prima Pils
STYLE
German Pilsner
ABV
5.3 %

I've always been a fan of Victory beers

The quality is tops

The aroma!

And you can find it everywhere!

Not to mention multiple brewing facilities and brewpubs across Southeastern PA

Parkesburg, PA

Can brew 2000 barrels DAILY

WHOA

Prima Pils is their year-round German pilsner

You know at family events when your Uncle says...

I only like beer that tastes like "beer"

Prima Pils looks like "beer" - it's straw colored, filtered, and frankly-looks kind of boring

But fresh German pils like Prima are a cut above this so-called "beer"

Prima Pils is woody, floral...

Hey Em!

deep breath

Morning!

...Like hiking on a chilly spring morning

That crisp nature comes from German or "noble" hops

oh wow!

It's like beer but... better! More complex!

What else is like this?

Another convert! Way to go Prima!

Best in a Tulip!

BREWERY
Ommegang
Cooperstown, NY
NAME
Witte
STYLE
Witbier
ABV
5.2 %

Ommegang is a Belgian style brewery in Cooperstown, NY

Their witte is summer in a glass

Wow- what a beautiful brewery

Witbiers are wheat beers brewed with with spices...

Like... Orange peel and coriander

Very subtle

Light

A beer made for urban or rural picnics

Refreshing

Soft

Pair with bright, fresh cuisine

Quaffable

A visit to Ommegang also means you're near the Baseball Hall of Fame!

Let's look at that beautiful Cooperstown scenery one more time

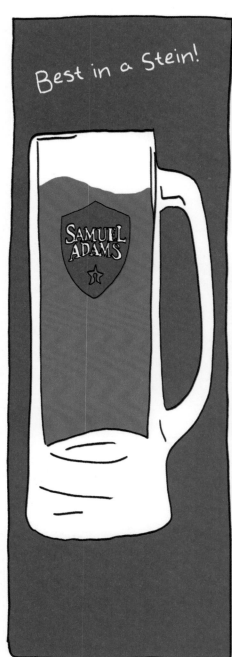

Best in a Stein!

Sorry Mom

Totally sorry

This was my friend Sean and I's drink of choice when we were underage

Boston Beer IS an original in the scene

The brewery was founded in 1984

Over 30 years ago!

Their Octoberfest is a classic

Stein suitable

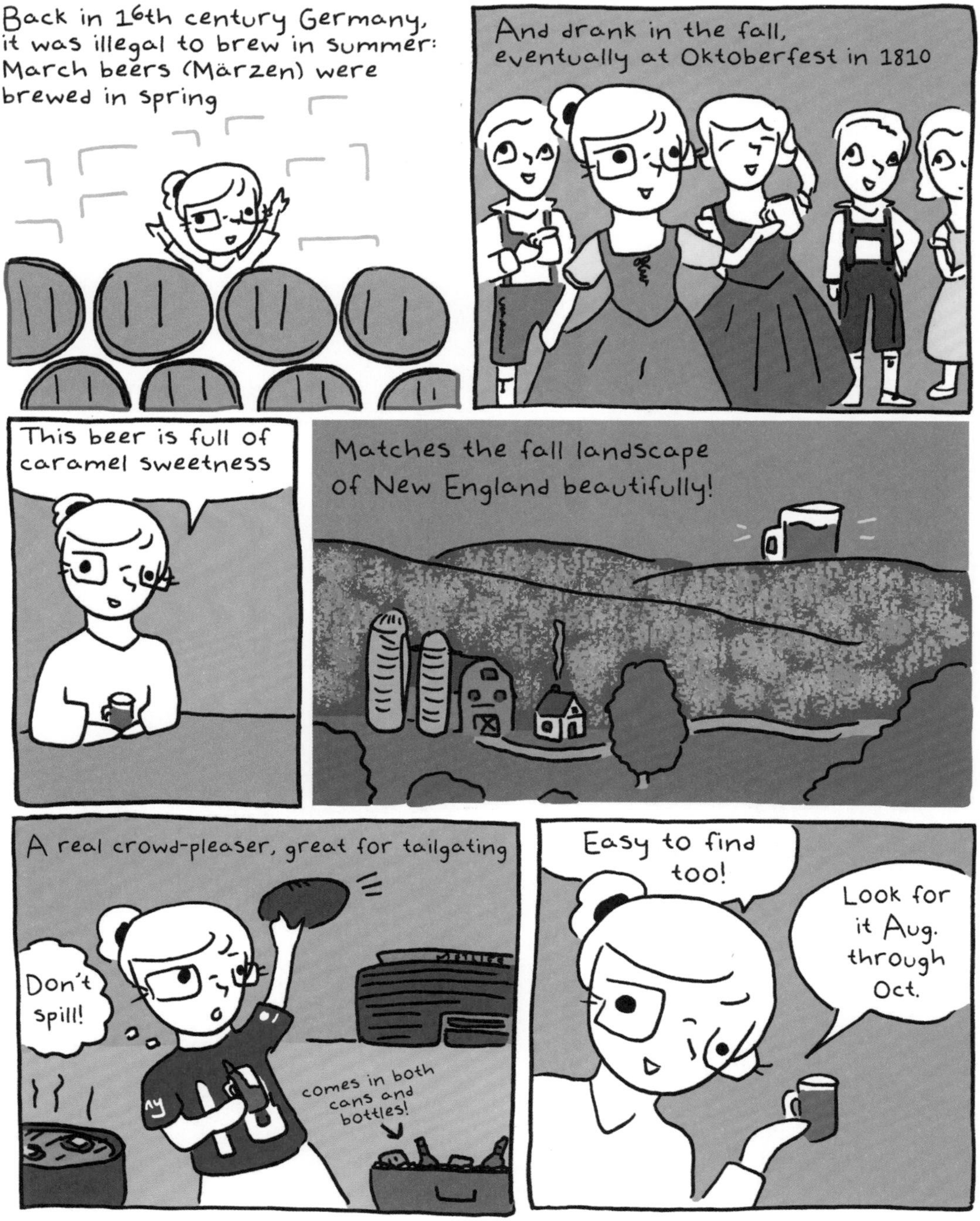
Back in 16th century Germany, it was illegal to brew in summer: March beers (Märzen) were brewed in spring
And drank in the fall, eventually at Oktoberfest in 1810
This beer is full of caramel sweetness
Matches the fall landscape of New England beautifully!
A real crowd-pleaser, great for tailgating
Don't spill!
comes in both cans and bottles!
Easy to find too!
Look for it Aug. through Oct.

Best in a Nonic!

BREWERY
Deschutes
Bend, OR
NAME
Black Butte
STYLE
Porter
ABV
5.2 %

The Sisters Volcanoes -
Bend, Oregon

Bend is an
amazing beer
town!

A must visit

Plus an outdoor
sports paradise

The largest brewery
in town (by far) is
Deschutes

Dang!

And they make an
amazing porter

Porters were the first mass-produced beer

cough
cough

Thanks to the industrial
revolution!

And named for the porters who
loved to stop for a pint during
their rounds

With its tan foam
and rich malt...

...it's
actually
refreshing

Yes!

Black beers
can be
light-bodied
and easy
to drink!

They aren't
always dense
and thick

Best for all manner
of Oregon weather

Be it
rain

snow

Or the occasional
sunny day on
the coast

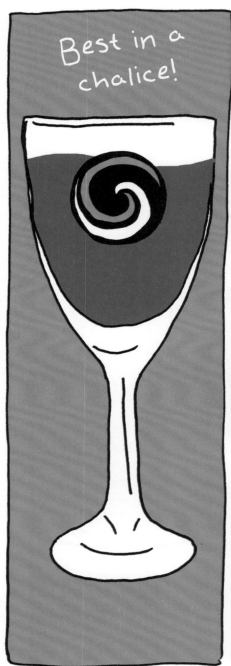

Best in a chalice!

BREWERY
Two Brothers
Warrenville, IL
NAME
Domaine DuPage
STYLE
Bière de Garde
ABV
5.9%

Ah, the beautiful French countryside

A French/Belgian style is Bière de Garde

Meaning "beer to keep"

Good to age or drink fresh

Two Brothers makes great beers

in Illinois

Including an award winning Bière de Garde- Domaine DuPage

Tastes like a basement

But that's what you want!

Mineral, toast- these are positives!

Trust me- a cartoon character!

Pairs well with Monet style haystacks!

And heavier fare

Bière de gardes are also great beers for the Holiday season

Leave for santa in place of milk

Joyeaux Noël all!

Best in a Snifter!

BREWERY
Hoppin' Frog
Akron, OH
NAME
B.O.R.I.S. the Crusher
STYLE
Russian Imperial Stout
ABV
9.4%

Ohio's Hoppin' Frog Brewery loves high alcohol brews

Many are 7% and up!

And most are easy to find at your local store

My fav is B.O.R.I.S.

"Bodacious Oatmeal Russian Imperial Stout"

Oatmeal adds fuller body and creaminess to the beer

Cheers!

Quaker Approved!

Silky Smooth

Like a soulful jazz ballad

Flavors of booze and fruit

The perfect nightcap

Good for snowbound evenings

A beer you deserve in this fancy snifter

A whiskey alternative

To drink in fancy PJs

So go ahead— put your feet up

This beer is great to age

Always store bottles upright so the yeast settles at the bottom!

THE WORLD OF BEER!

Ingredients, Food Pairings and Other Fun Facts

Each of these sections will introduce you to a new aspect of the wide world of beer! From ingredients to food pairings and more, let me guide you on an exploration of one of the world's best-loved drinks!

Water

Water may flow from a tap...

...But it's the backbone of beer

After all, in many places back in the day, beer was the only means of hydration

Water can add character thanks to calcium carbonate

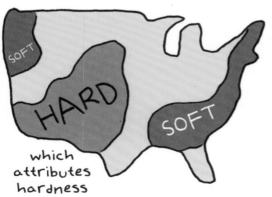

SOFT

HARD

SOFT

which attributes hardness

Soft water creates a pillowy texture

Perfect for pale lagers

Hard water is best for pale ales and dark beers

Great for bitter beers!

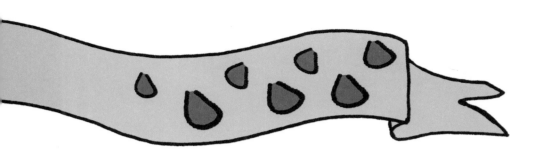

Water can make all sorts of beers

DUH

And of course, beer is refreshing

Perfect for the beach

Perfect for outdoors

Good for social functions or parties

you made it!

Yes and obviously I have beer

Grab your cooler and let's talk about refreshing beers!

BREWERY
New Glarus
New Glarus, WI
NAME
Spotted Cow
STYLE
Cream Ale
ABV
4.8%   Refreshing!

This quirky structure is a brewery

Despite only being sold in Wisconsin...

...New Glarus is one of the largest breweries in the U.S.

To me... ...this beer IS Wisconsin!

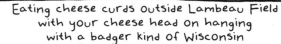

Eating cheese curds outside Lambeau Field with your cheese head on hanging with a badger kind of Wisconsin

Why are they squeaky?

They just are

Light, inoffensive

Easy to drink

An all-around crowd pleaser- even if it doesn't fit one singular beer style

oh what's this

Spotted Cow

It's a cream ale?

A farmhouse ale?

Who cares! We drink what we like!

Well- what is it then?

Spotted cow comes in can or bottle- Whatever your pleasure!

Doesn't matter what it is- it's GOOD

The right beer for the right situation is whatever you deem it to be!

BREWERY
Narragansett
Pawtucket, Rhode Island
NAME
Del's
STYLE
Shandy
ABV
4.7%   Refreshing!

A shandy is a British drink first written about in the 1850's...

Let's mix ginger beer and ale, Love

Smashing!

Most modern U.S. shandies are lemonade or lemon soda and beer

There's one shandy from a famous old school brewery

From Rhode Island...

FAMOUS for being filmed with a shark

crush

While Gansett's lager is still as popular as it was in JAWS

That will pair well with Quint

It's their shandy that's a popular summer beer

Plus- the lemon is from Del's

Del's

whose ice is summer in a cup

Quite possibly the best beach beer

Del's

The lemon blends well with this brew

Pair with Rhode Island mischief like peeking over Taylor Swift's fence on Watch Hill

!!

HEY YOU

Or legal fun like sunsets over Little Compton

BREWERY
Uinta
Salt Lake City, UT
NAME
Ready Set
STYLE
Gose
ABV Refreshing!
4%

Leipzig, Germany -
A cosmopolitan city
south of Berlin

Lovely
Old
Town
Hall!

Their love of gose made the
style a phenomenon

Say it
with me:

Gose:
Go-zah

Gose is a low ABV
ale brewed with
lactic acid & spices

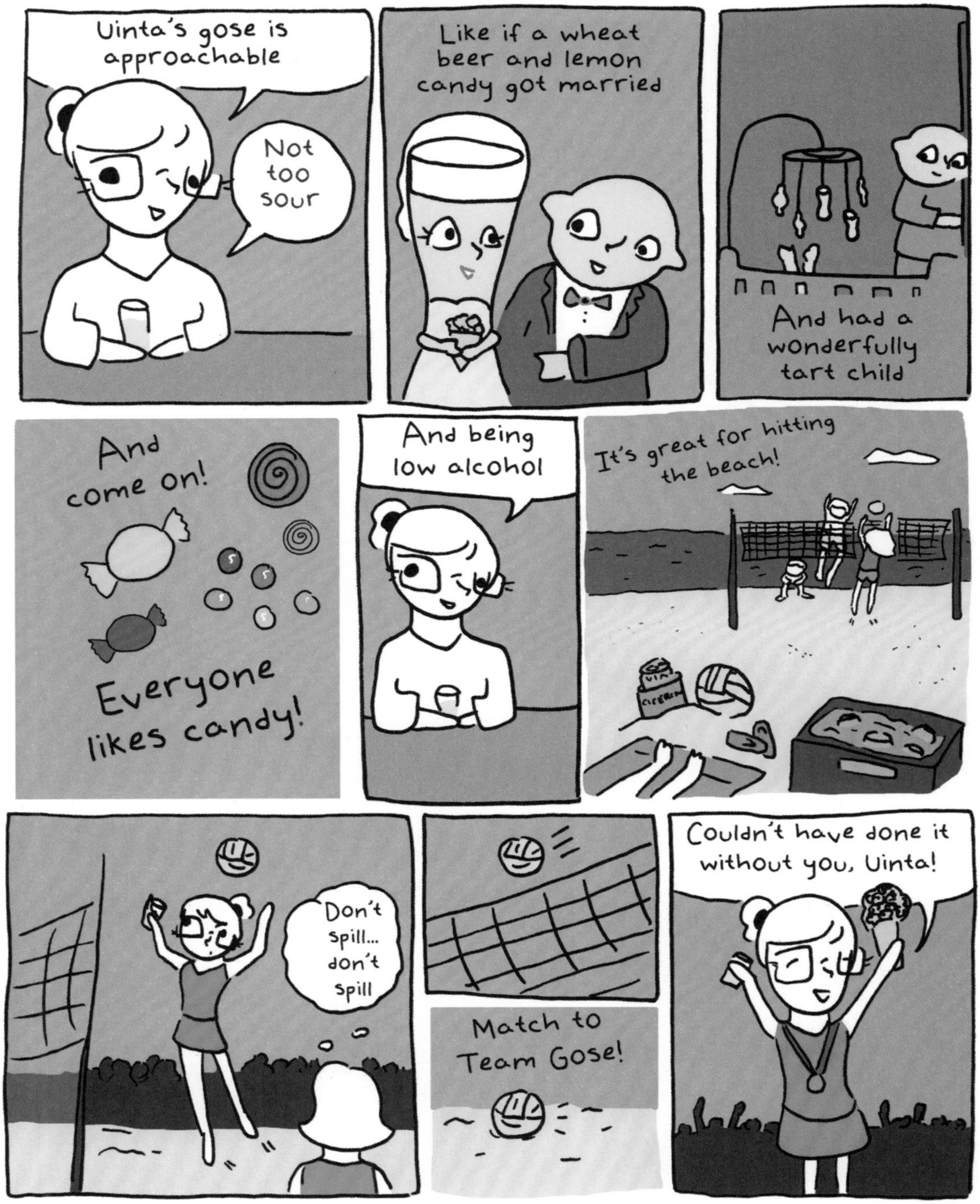
Uinta's gose is approachable
Not too sour
Like if a wheat beer and lemon candy got married
And had a wonderfully tart child
And come on!
Everyone likes candy!
And being low alcohol
It's great for hitting the beach!
Don't spill... don't spill
Match to Team Gose!
Couldn't have done it without you, Uinta!

BREWERY
Ska
Durango, CO
NAME
Pils World Craft Lager
STYLE
German Pilsner
ABV
5.4% Refreshing!

Ska Brewing only uses cans for their brews

CANS ARE
*Transportable
*Let no light in
*keep beer fresh!

Using cans makes sense given their locale in the Rocky Mts

Their pils is fresh&grassy

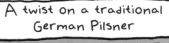
A twist on a traditional German Pilsner

Which means it's more fruity on the finish

Very American

Perfect for day trips around Durango

Mesa Verde National Park

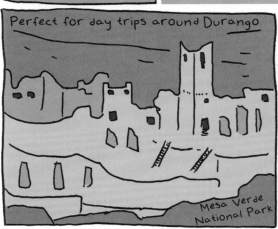

Or scaling "14ers" like the nearby Wisdom Peak

I'm in over my head here

PANT PANT

Like spicy food? This beer will help beat the heat!

I'm in over my head here

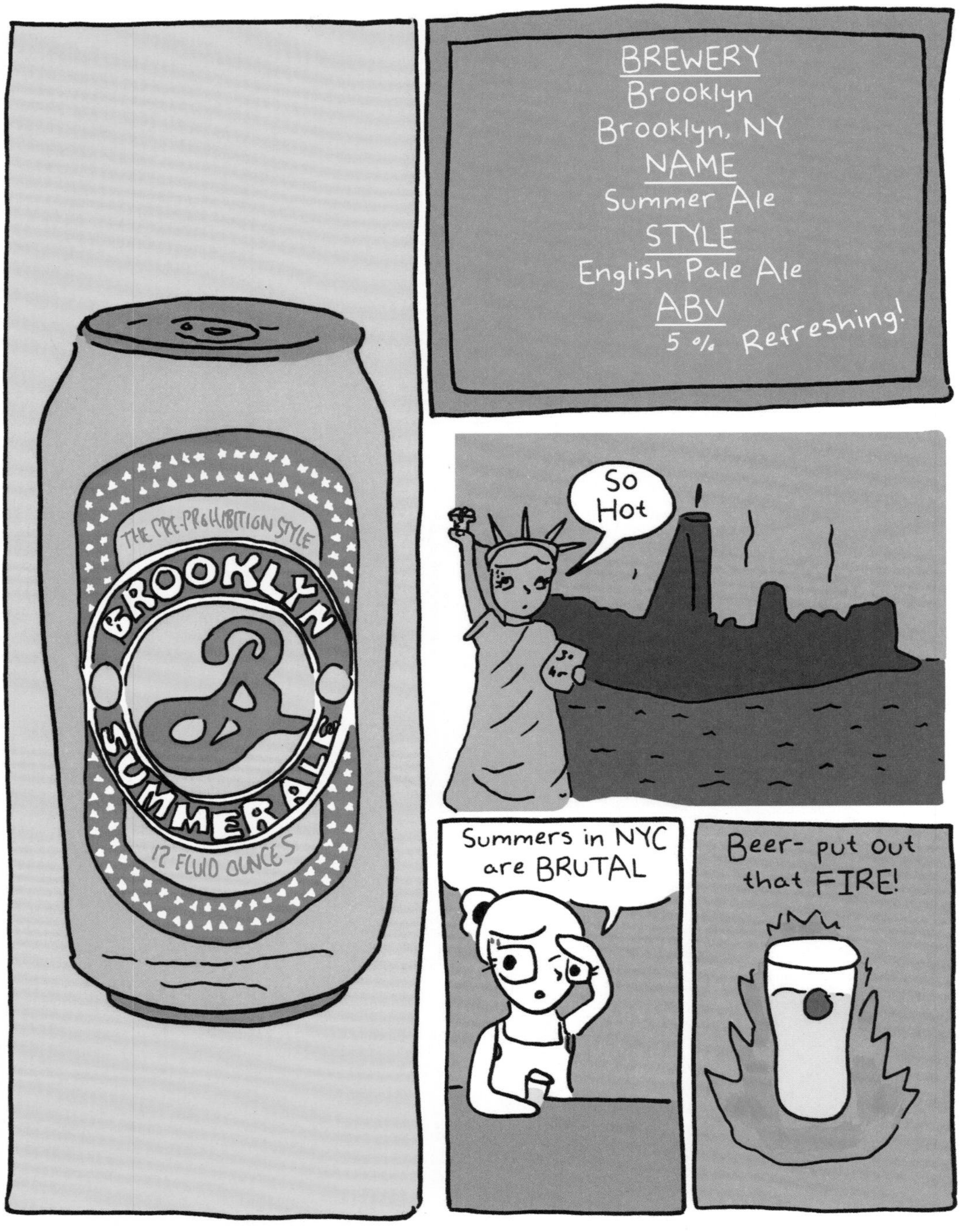
THE PRE-PROHIBITION STYLE
BROOKLYN
SUMMER ALE
12 FLUID OUNCES
BREWERY
Brooklyn
Brooklyn, NY
NAME
Summer Ale
STYLE
English Pale Ale
ABV
5 %
Refreshing!
So Hot
Summers in NYC are BRUTAL
Beer- put out that FIRE!

Enter Brooklyn Brewery

Me trying to look hip

Could it be the most refreshing beer on Earth?

Maybe!

Remember the beer you drank in college?

It's like that...

But Better

Light corn sweetness

A Goldilocks brew

Sweet, not too sweet

Just right

Like fresh cut flowers!

Lovely floral aroma

Best for Brooklyn summer activities

Beach @ Coney Is.

Dumpster Swimming

Twilight Rooftops

It's summer

It's beer

Life is good

Malt

Malt creates beer's color and adds sweetness

Grain is steeped in water and then dried to lock in sugar

2 Row

6 Row

Breweries use 2 row and 6 row barley

Classic European malt house

Then kilned to a specific color

Malt creates many colors in beer from light to dark

which can be measured!

The Standard Reference Model (SRM) measures color in beer

Pale Lager
Pale Ale
Saison
Bière de Garde
Amber Ale
Brown Ale
Porter
Imperial Stout

= 3

= 13

= 30

SRM is a number system that ranges from 3 to 40+

That's why beer is called "liquid bread"

Sugars in the malt feed the yeast that create CO_2 and alcohol

Beer that rely on malt as its primary flavor tend to be sweeter in nature

Like cereal or baked goods

Do you like baked goods?

Of course you do!

From scotch ales to brown ales and beyond

All the sugar hiding away in those kernals

simple sugars!

helps feed the yeast!

So malt has TWO uses!

Malt is the soul of beer

BREWERY
Great Lakes
Cleveland, OH
NAME
Edmund Fitzgerald
STYLE
Porter
ABV
6 %

Malty!

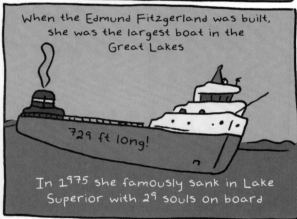

When the Edmund Fitzgerland was built, she was the largest boat in the Great Lakes

729 ft long!

In 1975 she famously sank in Lake Superior with 29 souls on board

Superior - they said never gives up her dead ♫

Mr. Gordon Lightfoot everyone!

Beers can be a fitting tribute

Good to remember those we lost

The bell chimed... 29 times

Don't let the color fool you

Porters are lighter-bodied and can be refreshing

And they are smooth like a quiet day on the lakes

Roasty flavors like bitter chocolate or black coffee

A good beer for ice fishing

Or even regular ole fishing!

A beer for all seasons

The legend lives on from the Chippewa on down...

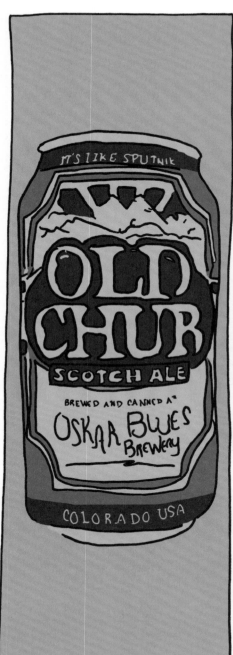

BREWERY
Oskar Blues
Lyons, CO
NAME
Old Chub
STYLE
Scotch Ale
ABV
8 %

Malty!

Scotland is known for liquor- but they also make great beer

After all, barley is a chief export of Scotland

One of the best scotch ales or "wee heavy" ales comes from a cutting edge brewery

In the early 2000's, Oskar Blues changed everything

As one of the first to can microbrewed beer

DALE PALE ALE

Gika Blue

And they can everything

So cool

A canned scotch ale!

Scotch ales are BIG MALT

Like drinking a really fancy dark loaf of bread

Beautiful light banana and plum features

Hint of smoke for you scotch whiskey drinkers

A great rain day in your castle overlooking a loch kind of beer

Brr

Don't forget to share with magical creatues

wow

S.S. NESSIE

Or keep it for yourself— it's your life

BREWERY
Left Hand
Longmont, CO
NAME & STYLE
Nitro Milk Stout
ABV
6 %

Malty!

What does a beer mean when it's "nitro?"

I'm not talking about "American Gladiators"

Ooh

I'm talking Nitrogen gas

N$_2$

Normal Draft Beer

50% or more CO_2

Nitro Draft Beer

75% N$_2$

25% CO_2

Left Hand was one of the first smaller breweries...

...to add nitrogen to bottles. A big deal when it debuted!

N_2

So what's the difference?

OH YEAH

Nitrogen bubbles are smaller and lighter so the taste has a velvet smooth consistency

that's called mouthfeel

Plus, milk stouts are brewed with milk sugar or lactose

which also adds texture

↑ This all mingles nicely with the roasted malt

Essentially this beer is like a velvet gown...

...you want to drink!

Best enjoyed while sledding

not literally

Or pair with cookies for an adult version of a classic

And on behalf of all dairy cows- we are thrilled to be included in such a stellar product

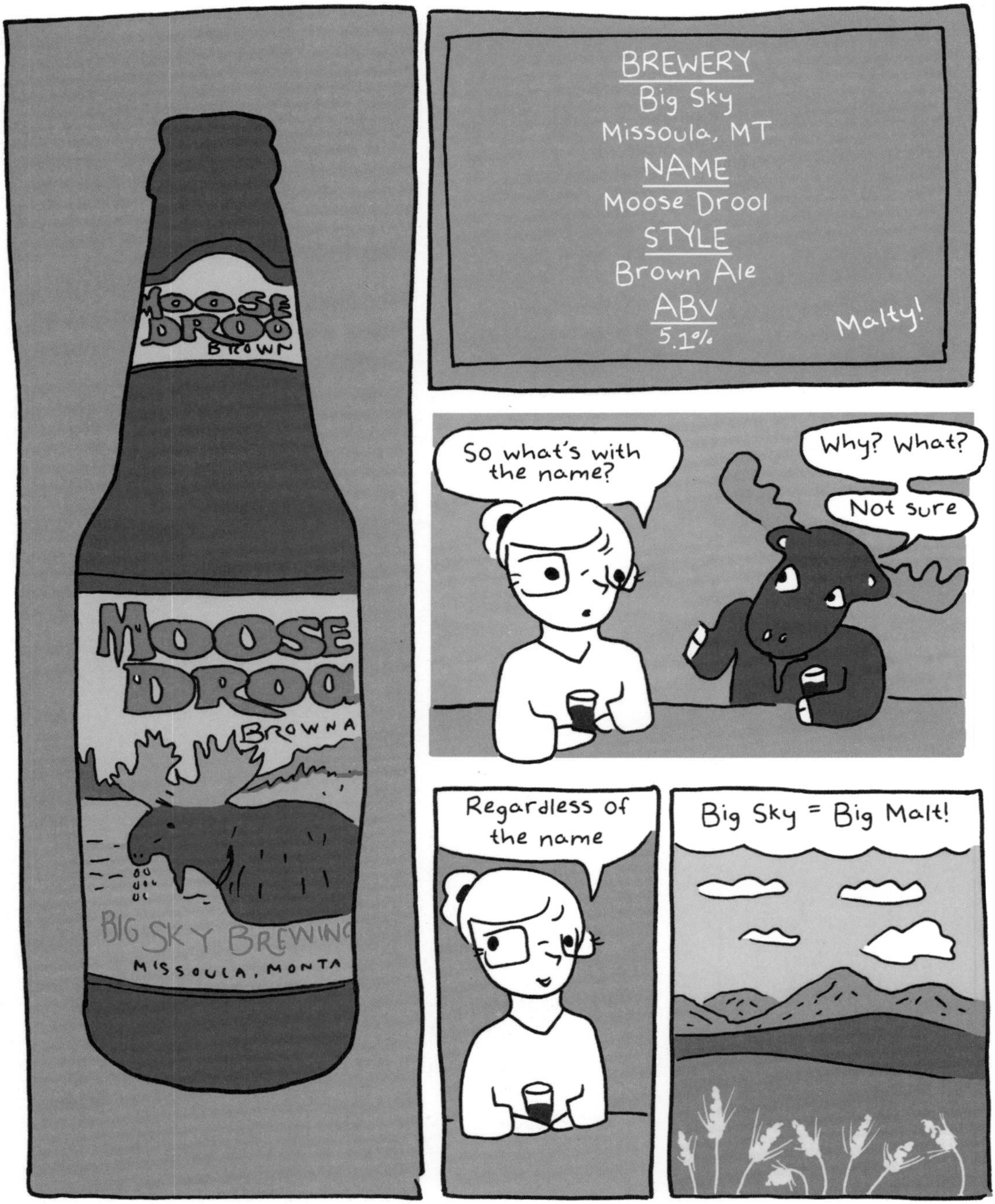
MOOSE
BROWN
BREWERY
Big Sky
Missoula, MT
NAME
Moose Drool
STYLE
Brown Ale
ABV
5.1%
Malty!
So what's with the name?
Why? What?
Not sure
Regardless of the name
Big Sky = Big Malt!

The aroma is roasty-like a cup of coffee

But it's an easy drinker

Full of caramel sweetness

Available in both can and bottle plus very easy to find on the West Coast make a solid, heartier option for exploring America's national treasures

Wow

Whoa

mmm

Pair with a fresh elk burger- yum!

Cousin Billings?!

GASP!

...

BREWERY
Anchor
San Francisco, CA
NAME
Anchor Steam
STYLE
California Common
ABV
4.9 %

Steam beer is a wholly American beer style

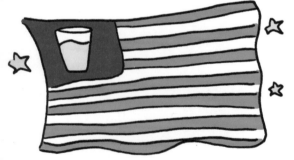

And historically associated with the West Coast and San Fran!

California Common or "Steam Beer" is a lager that is fermented at warmer temps.

Historically, The open fermentation tanks sat on the roof, and evaporated over the city, hence the

{ STEAM }

Made in SF since it was first brewed in 1896

Fresh Anchor Steam smells like dough wafting from a bakery

HOPS

Hops were first used in beer in the Middle Ages

YUP

Before that time, beer was bittered and flavored with a mixture of herbs/plants called gruit

mugwort

yarrow

Heather

Ivy

Hops were once used as salad greens

And as medicine...

insomnia

anxiety

stomach ailments

They were discovered to have preservative qualities

written in detail by Abbess Hildegarde of Germany in 1150

Keeping beer fresher longer? A good notion for people who relied on beer to survive

Thanks hops for keeping beer fresh!

I can now live to be 40!

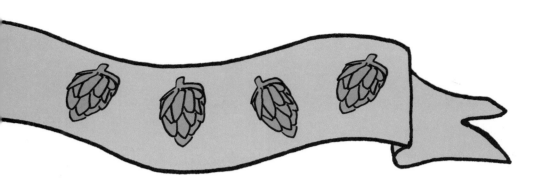

Hops grow on trellises about 18-20 ft. tall in the US & 21/22 ft. in Europe

In America, hops are harvested between Aug-Sept

Different countries are known for certain hops...

Pacific NW

← Cascade

England

← Fuggle

Germany

← Hallertau

New Zealand

← Nelson Sauvin

Hops contribute bitterness but also flavor to beer

Popular hops and their aromas

Citra............melon, grapefruit
Mosaic............blueberry, rose
Fuggle..........mint, grass, flowers
Saaz..................light spice, herbal
Cascade..........citrus, grapefruit
Hallertau..............earthy, herbal
Nelson Sauvin.......white wine
East Kent Golding..........lavender
Chinook........pine, grapefruit
Galaxy........passion fruit, citrus

What grapes are to wine...hops are for beer!

More than just bitter!

Brewed with Magnum, Perle & Cascade Hops

BREWERY
Sierra Nevada
Chico, CA
NAME AND STYLE
Pale Ale
ABV
5.6%

HOPPY!

This beer was first brewed in 1979 - can you dig it?

Sierra Nevada Pale Ale - a real original

A rock star, a celebrity

Drink me!

In a sea of taps...

You can rest assured that the Sierra Nevada Pale Ale will be consistent and of good quality

The flavor is old school

Malty with rich amber grains

The hop profile is good and earthy

Easy to drink

Easy to love

This beer has the respect of an entire industry

And perfect for camping when in cans

This was one of my gateway beers into craft

2006 me!

Thank you Sierra Nevada for your years of service to beer and tastiness

Brewed with
Centennial Hops!

Two Hearted
Ale

...Pale Ale with intense hop aroma.

BREWERY
Bell's
Kalamazoo, MI
NAME
Two Hearted
STYLE
India Pale Ale
ABV
7%   HOPPy!

The Two Hearted River
flows through the Upper
Peninsula of Michigan

That's where this
beer gets its name

Plus Michigan
has a fine
brewing tradition

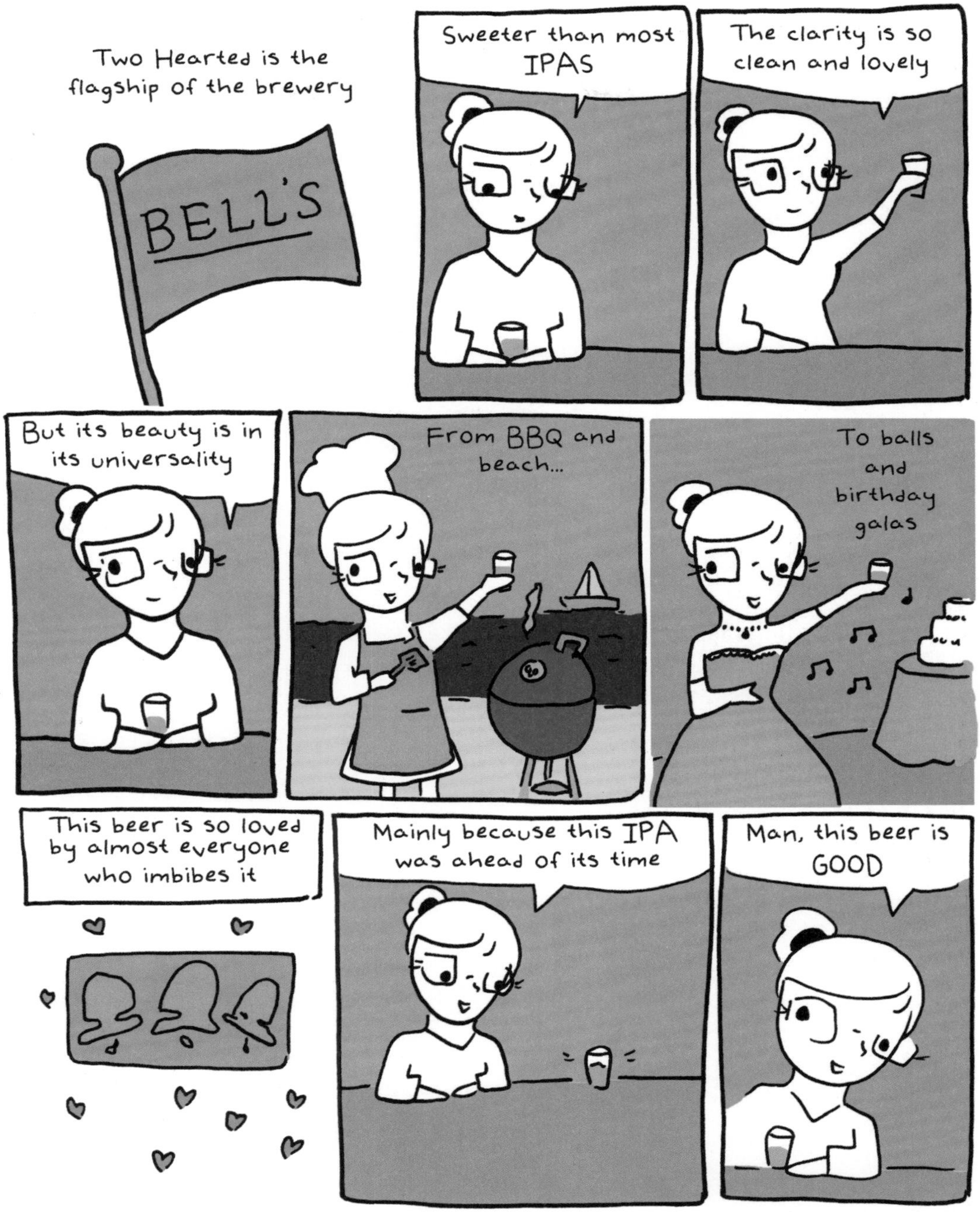

Two Hearted is the flagship of the brewery
BELL'S
Sweeter than most IPAS
The clarity is so clean and lovely
But its beauty is in its universality
From BBQ and beach...
To balls and birthday galas
This beer is so loved by almost everyone who imbibes it
Mainly because this IPA was ahead of its time
Man, this beer is GOOD

Brewed with Centennial, Chinook, Columbus, and other hop varietals

BREWERY
Ballast Point
San Diego, CA
NAME
Grapefruit Sculpin
STYLE
India Pale Ale
ABV   HOPPY!
7 %

Ballast Point started as many breweries have started...

still open →   HOME BREW MART

...as a homebrew shop

Now Ballast Point is a major brewery

Who changed the IPA forever when they added grapefruit

to their most popular beer

Hops can impart tons of different flavors

Citrus for one

But what if we added citrus fruit directly to the IPA?

And thus the fruited IPA craze was BORN

This beer is as revolutionary...

...as it is delicious

If you like grapefruit, then this beer is for you! ♥

Citrus rind character

So Fresh

This beer connects the dots — the meeting of bitter, fruity and juicy

No IPAs!

Trade ya!

Give it a go

Oh Whoa!

This is AWESOME!

Ok give it back

Give what back?

Oh man! Well, it's the price I pay

Brewed with Warrior, Ahtanum, Cascade, Simcoe, & Amarillo Hops

FOR A GLASS, FROM A CAN

SURLY FURIOUS BEER
1 PINT

BREWERY
Surly
Brooklyn Center, MN
NAME
Furious
STYLE
India Pale Ale
ABV
6.7 %

HOPPY!

When traveling in Minnesota...

...It's hard to go anywhere and not see Surly Brewing

Oh hey!

Hey Em

!!!

HEY!

Their IPA is called Furious

It's an IPA that's more malt focused

The beer has a chewy, cereal-like appeal

That's a good thing

IPAs nowadays - the hop is the star

But with this beer- hops and malt share the stage

The bitter finish lingers pleasantly

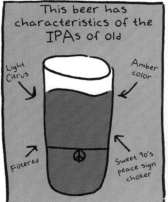

This beer has characteristics of the IPAs of old

Light Citrus

Amber color

Filtered

Sweet 90's peace sign choker

All the while calling back the British beer tradition

Thanks Surly for creating a beer that looks to the past and the future

Brewed with Chinook, Centennial, and Amarillo Hops!

BECAUSE BEER MATTERS

FREMONT

INTERURBAN

IPA

FREMONT BREWING

BECAUSE BEER MATTERS

BREWERY
Fremont
Seattle, WA
NAME
Interurban
STYLE
India Pale Ale
ABV
6.2 %

HOPPY!

Fremont opened its doors in 2009

But it feels more old school than that

yes!

Maybe it's the timeless label design

Or the deep affinity they have for their hometown of Seattle

Their IPA is of the West Coast style

West Coast IPAs are valued for their heavy pine and citrus notes

Fremont's IPA is also balanced with its use of amber malts

Along with a delightful grassy finish

It also has a finish that is "resinous"

Like a hop leaving footprints on your tongue after each sip!

I'm walking on sunshine!

This beer captures the spirit of the Pacific Northwest

Pair with beautiful hikes along Puget Sound

Yeast

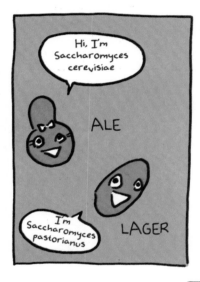

Hi, I'm Saccharomyces cerevisiae

ALE

I'm Saccharomyces pastorianus

LAGER

We are yeast, and we make

BEER!

We are the ultimate beer geeks

Without us, no booze!

Back in ancient times, beer was fermented naturally with wild yeast in the air

Yum

In the late 19th century, Emil Hansen isolated yeast strains

Emil C. Hansen

No Biggie

Now a brewery could brew a saison one day...

And a lager the next

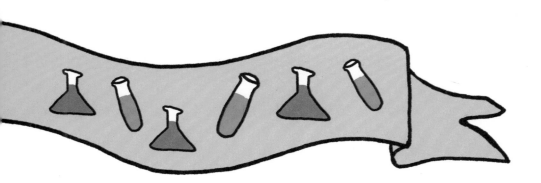

We feast on the sugar in the fermenting beer

Delicious! Yum!

munch munch

BURP

SORRY

and burp up CO_2 and alcohol

Certain yeast strains create different beers

I take two weeks at 68F

I take four weeks at 48F

Yeast can also create flavorful byproducts - esters & phenols

banana

pear

GUM

ESTERS

clove

barnyard

PHENOLS

YEEHAW

There are also WILD yeast strains- they make beer funky and sour

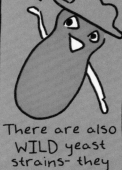

We love what we do

burp and eat- yup!

BREWERY
Hardywood
Richmond, VA
NAME
Singel
STYLE
Belgian Blonde Ale
ABV
6.2 %

Yeasty!

Belgian monks love their beer!

And many breweries are still monk run

Or "Trappist" Breweries

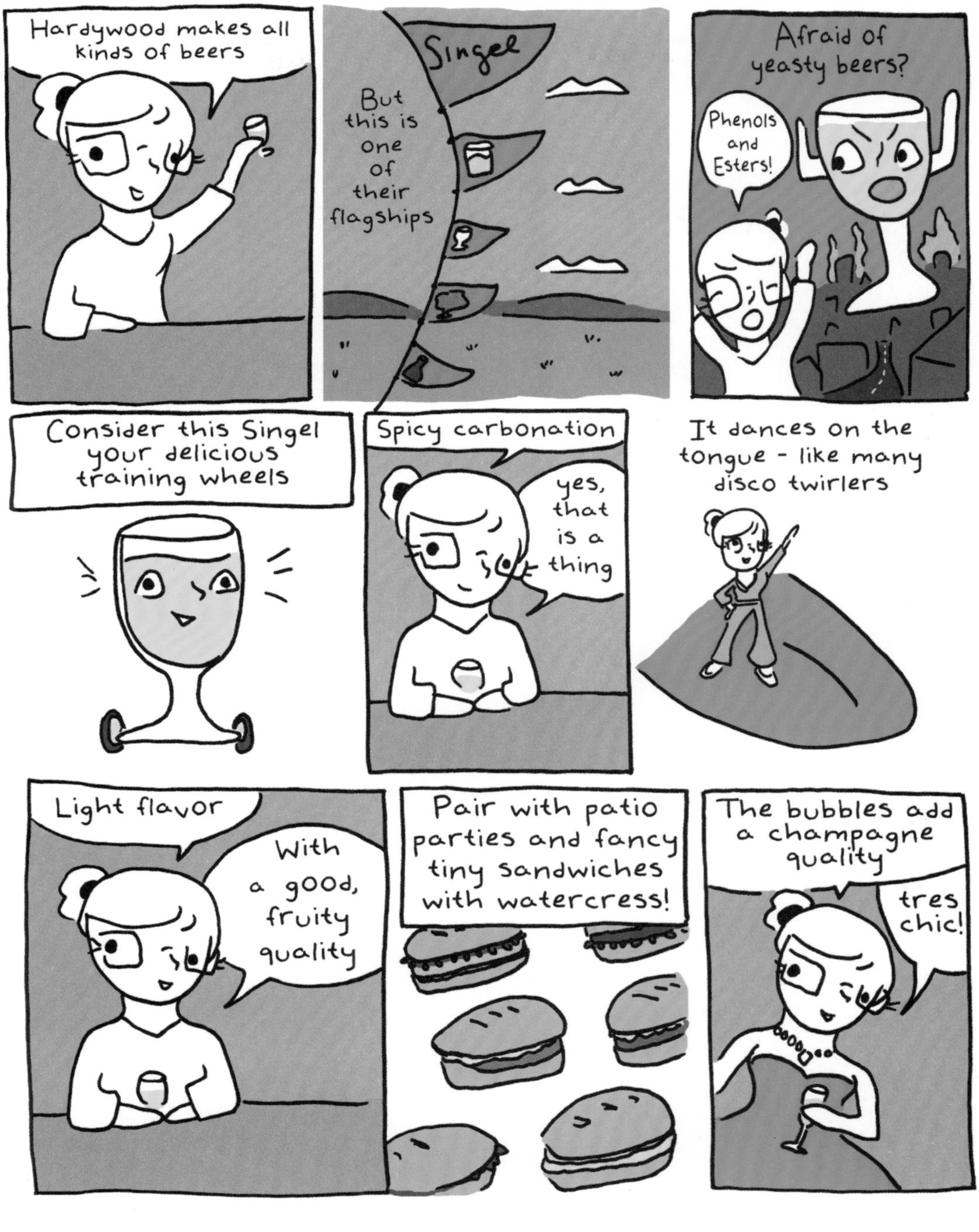
Hardywood makes all kinds of beers
Singel
But this is one of their flagships
Afraid of yeasty beers?
Phenols and Esters!
Consider this Singel your delicious training wheels
Spicy carbonation
yes, that is a thing
It dances on the tongue - like many disco twirlers
Light flavor
With a good, fruity quality
Pair with patio parties and fancy tiny sandwiches with watercress!
The bubbles add a champagne quality
tres chic!

BREWERY
Perennial Artisan Ales
St. Louis, MO
NAME
Saison De Lis
STYLE
Saison
ABV
5 %

Yeasty!

Back in the day, Belgian farm workers received beer as payment

The beer was made with whatever they had in the barn

Including restorative herbs like chamomile

Similar to traditional saisons

But it's boozier than what came before

Excellent flavors of melon plus minerality

Yes, rocks!

Sometimes you want beer to have an almost dirty character

soil-esque

It's a good thing

White wine drinkers

The mineral notes are reminiscent of a pinot gris

Also fruity sweet - like gummy bears!

This saison is a wonderful addition to a big dinner

Is that wine?   Nope!

Love the label, is it cider?

Just try it

Think of white wine as you sip

Ooh!

If you mention the flavors before people take a sip, it's easier to find them!

So good! Thanks!   You're welcome!

BREWERY
Allagash
Portland, ME
NAME & STYLE
Tripel
ABV
9 %
Yeasty!

In 1995 Rob Tod opened Allagash Brewing Company

Their flagship White Ale is hugely popular

Because it is incredibly delicious!

Their Belgian style beers are as fresh and as lovely as a Maine morning

Pretty as a picture

Their tripel is super fruity

Kinda reminds me of a wine but I'm not sure which one

Ah ha!

Let's ask a wine expert!

He'll know the perfect thing to say

Like a rich chenin blanc from Savennieres in the Loire Valley, honeyed but not sweet, charmingly brash

Jameson Fink, Editor at Wine Enthusiast

Yeah

What he said

Crazy to think all that flavor comes mainly from yeast!

Thanks all!

Just doing our jobs

Pair with hearty New England style fare, like a pot pie

Also- mind the alcohol- similar to wine at a hefty 9 % ABV

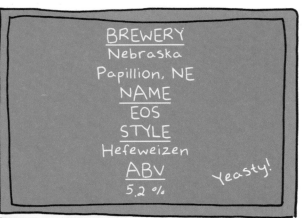

BREWERY
Nebraska
Papillion, NE
NAME
EOS
STYLE
Hefeweizen
ABV
5.2 %

Yeasty!

Fresh banana bread!

What if I told you there is a beer

that mimics the flavors of banana & clove?

Enter Nebraska Brewing EOS Hef

What if I told you that **flavor was from the yeast!**

The same chemical compound found in banana flavored candy!

The clove and banana tastes in this beer is

BIG!

This banana and clove pair well with the soft, pillowy wheat beer base...like a dream

Super well made

An amazing brunch beer

A splash of OJ in this beer will make you forget mimosas

Bon Appetit!

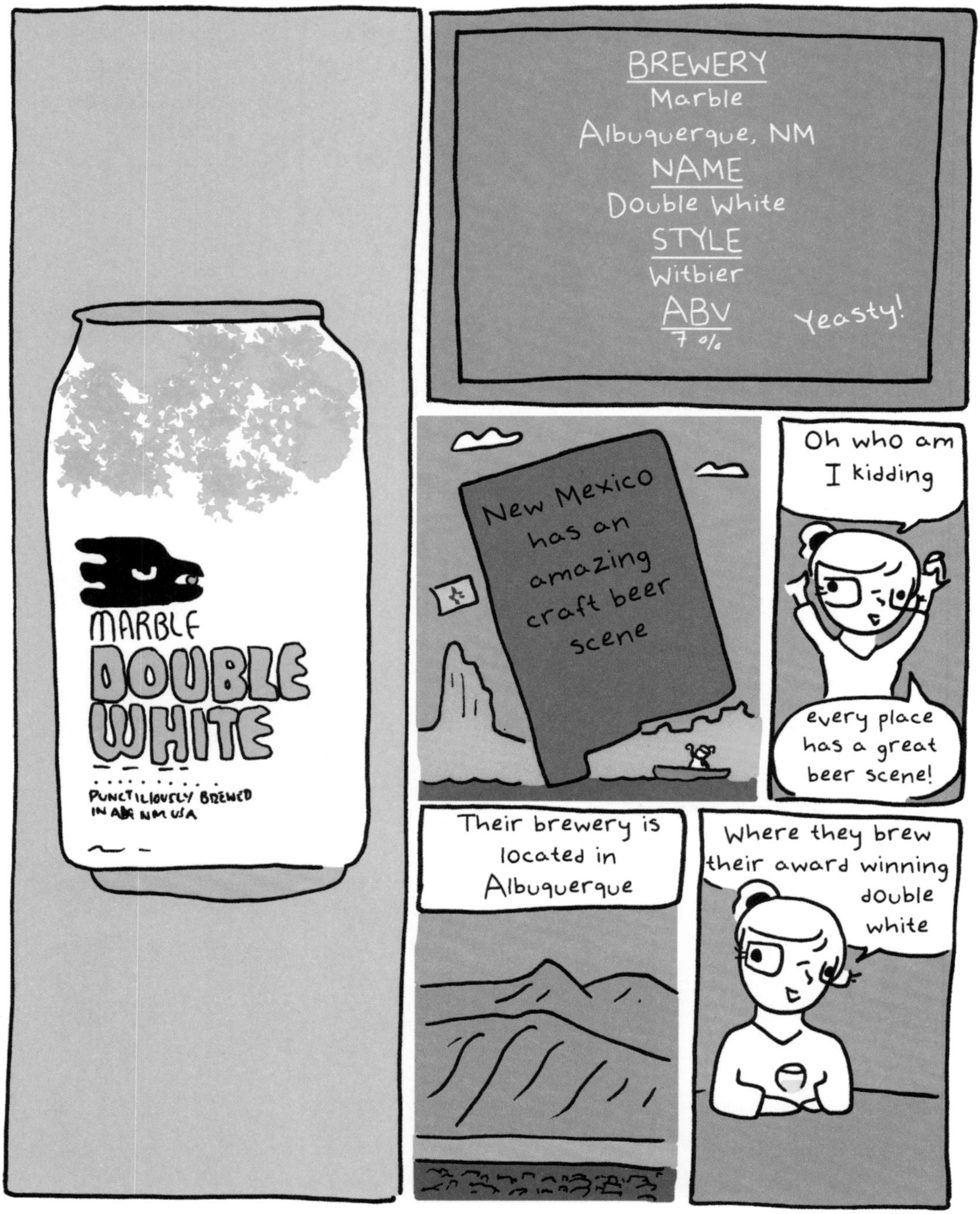
MARBLE
DOUBLE WHITE
PUNCTILIOUSLY BREWED IN ABQ NM USA
BREWERY
Marble
Albuquerque, NM
NAME
Double White
STYLE
Witbier
ABV
7 %
Yeasty!
New Mexico has an amazing craft beer scene
Oh who am I kidding
every place has a great beer scene!
Their brewery is located in Albuquerque
Where they brew their award winning double white

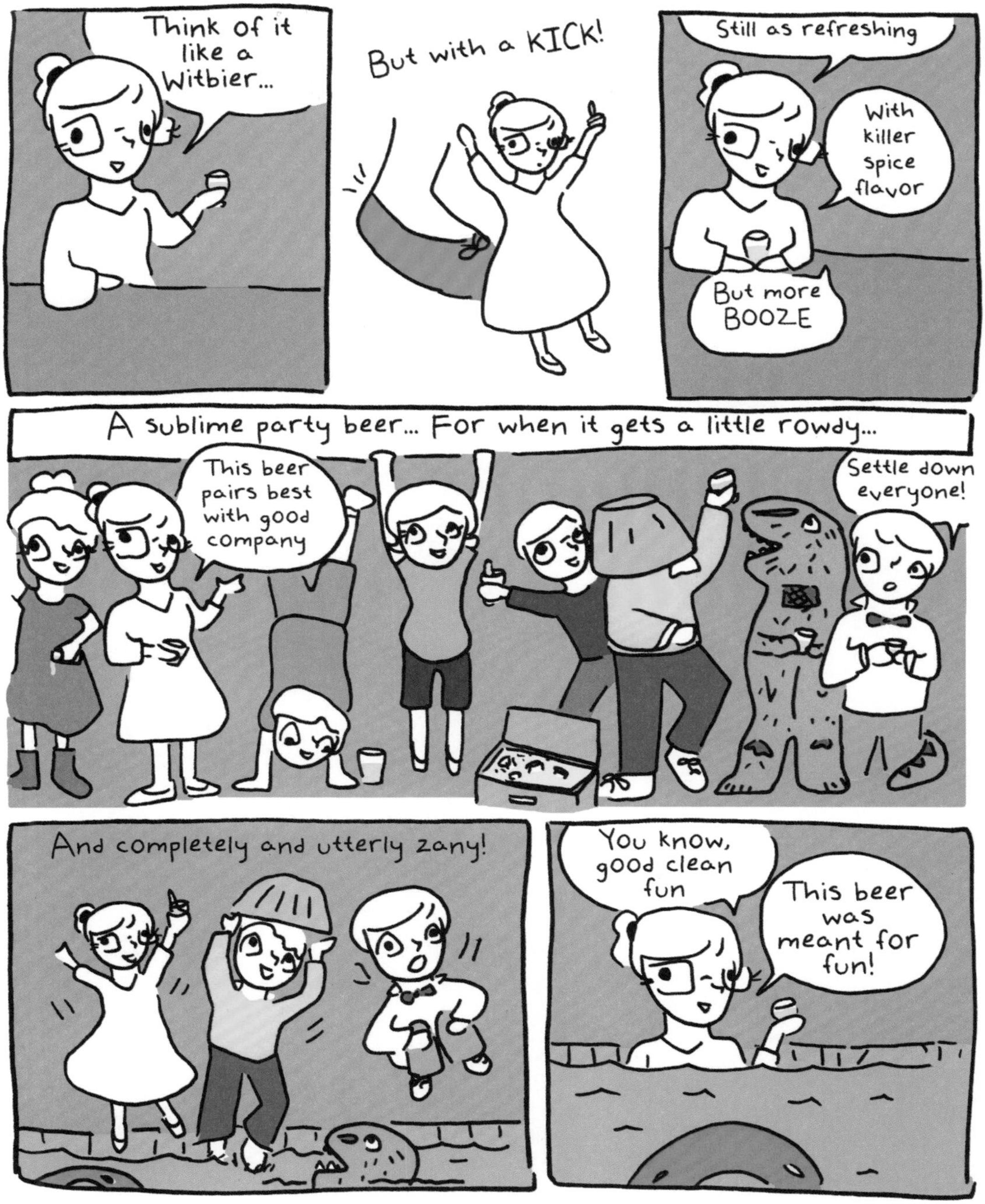
Think of it like a Witbier...
But with a KICK!
Still as refreshing
With killer spice flavor
But more BOOZE
A sublime party beer... For when it gets a little rowdy...
This beer pairs best with good company
Settle down everyone!
And completely and utterly zany!
You know, good clean fun
This beer was meant for fun!

Experimental

MALT

WATER

YEAST

HOPS

In America we are not defined by these ingredients

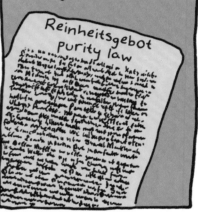

If you live in Germany though, it's the law!

Reinheitsgebot Purity law

Here in the U.S. — we'll brew with pretty much anything we can get our hands on

Mushrooms! Lime! Spices! Honey! Basil!

OLD BAY SEASONING

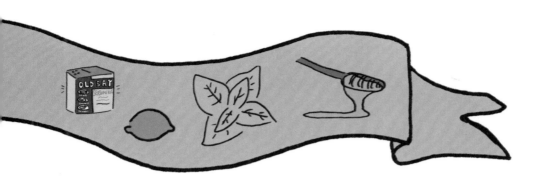

Brewing in America is about creativity

Wow! What Color

Curry is delicious! Wait- what about curry in a beer!?!?

The experimentation

And melding of art and science

With experimentation - whole styles are born!

 Black IPA
Vermont Pub and Brewery
1994

Dry-hopped sours
Done by many breweries since 2014

You never know what tinkering can create

A curry witbier?! Wow- this is great!

Inspiration is tantamount to beer

BREWERY
Fullsteam
Durham, NC
NAME
Southern Basil
STYLE
Saison
ABV
5 %   Experimental!

BASIL!

Wonderful aroma

But adding it to a saison?

You know, that could be interesting!

It does work for pasta...

And beer is a carbohydrate as well!

Basil plus a Belgian yeast strain

Tastes healthy and refreshing like a green salad

Vegetal and bright

It works so well

Pair the cans with a Fourth of July BBQ

Or share with fireflies

Ooh!

saison!

YES!

Let's share!

Hi! I'm a Maryland Crab

Let's be friends!

Crabs are big biz in Maryland

As is their famous spice- Old Bay

OLD BAY SEASONING

Sorry crab, nothing personal

it's cool

So Maryland-based Flying Dog made a beer with the popular spice

Don't worry— it doesn't taste like me!

The spice is restrained

But zesty!

The body is light...

Made to drink outside

CHESAPEAKE

Experimental...

But not scary

Approachable — which is good!

Obviously pair with binge watching HBO's The Wire

Oh dang, it's Omar!

Watch out Bodymore!

For food— pair with delicious Maryland blue crab...

Or grilled chicken!

BREWERY
Short's
Bellaire, MI
NAME
Melt My Brain
STYLE
Experimental Golden Ale
ABV
3.8% Experimental!

Cocktails-Classy!

Look at that crown!

Breweries are now experimenting with beer/cocktail hybrids

Michigan's Short's Brewing are masters of this trend

Owner Joe Short has a mad scientist mustache!

Short's has already created a White Russian beer

With a Big Lebowski theme

They call this a gin and tonic beer

How does that happen?

A blonde ale base with added ingredients

coriander

Juniper

Limes

Tonic water

fresh, cool

Love the low ABV too

Really tastes like a G&T!

Joe- you really are a mad scientist

MUAHAH HAHAHA Excellent!

Pair with spring cleaning and other tidying activities

Drink   Do not drink

Give to fun seniors that resemble the by-gone era of the Golden Girls

Ale?

Rue, try it

I do declare- THIS is beer?

Are there other beers like this?

Well, Brooklyn Brewing has an Old Fashioned beer and so does Wicked Weed. Flying Dog and Excel Brewing both brew Mint Julep beers. NoDa makes a mojito beer, then there are margarita beers, white russian beers, sazerac beers and lime rickey beers, whiskey sour beers, gin fizz beers, ETC

BREWERY
Scratch
Ava, IL
NAME AND STYLE
Chanterelle
Bière de Garde
ABV
6.3% Experimental!

Mushroom hunting...

This goofy looking shroom

is a chanterelle

Scratch Brewing makes a beer with this fungi

wait... what?!

Scratch is famous for its foraged beers

Which makes for interesting flavors

Super cool next level stuff

This biere de garde with chanterelle reminds me of soup

In a good way of course

Buttery and meaty

With a very rich malt backbone

Normally meat and butter are off-flavors

Sounds crazy- it really does

But it works!

A stay in bed kind of beer- almost feels restorative like tonics of old

Other groups like "Beers made by Walking" host lectures and brew beer from ingredients found on urban and rural walks

Eric Steen, founder of Beers made by Walking

The future of geekdom is here

BREWERY
Dogfish Head
Milton, DE
NAME
Midas Touch
STYLE
Spice Beer
ABV
9 % Experimental!

I love history!

Big book of stuff

This beer right here

IS made of history!

Dogfish Head took inspiration from ingredients found in the burial mound of the real King Midas in Turkey

Built 2700 years ago!

WHOA

Ancient brewing included honey, grapes, saffron...

Plus barley!

A hybrid of all liquors

This is some Indiana Jones stuff

But how does

it taste?

So unique!

Like a Belgian beer

Love that saffron!

A great dinner party beer- a fun wine alternative

Easy to find, pairs well with many foods, plus that backstory!

Did you know 2700 years ago...

Dogfish Head has always brewed outside the box- very cool

Old World

A plane ride to Europe can be expensive

$$$$$

Guess no oktoberfest this year

Luckily- I have a cheaper option than the grand tour

Although American breweries love to experiment

Needs more Lucky Charms

They also love the classics of the Old World

Lovely Altbier

Thanks!

After all, Europeans have been brewing for centuries

Bayerische Staatsbrauerei Weihenstephan-Freising, Germany. Founded in 1040

Most American styles started as European styles

Americans like to tinker with Euro styles:

MORE HOPS

WILD YEAST

BARREL AGING

↑
HIGHER ABV

Even though it looks like we are tampering with the classics

It's really an homage to the past!

Beer plays such a role in the culture of Europe

From the abbeys of Belgium...

From the industrialized brewing of the United Kingdom

open fermentation of ales circa 1890

To the alpen lands of Austria and Germany

We know what came before

Cheers! Prost! Slainte! Sante! Na Zdravi!

BREWERY
Firestone Walker
Paso Robles, CA
NAME
Pivo
STYLE
German Pilsner
ABV
5.3%
German!

Pilsners were all the rage in Europe in the 1800's

Magnifique!

Oui

tres bien

Loving the czech version...

...Germans adapted the recipe to suit their taste

German hops

Lighter and drier

And Firestone Walker took the German style and added a distinct American twist

They dry hop it

Adding dry hops to already fermenting beer

Adds extra flavor

Guten tag

Firestone Walker dry hops with German Saphir hops

Dry-hopping was a British invention FYI

So this beer is super old world

Dry-hopping adds unbelievable aroma moreso than a typical German style pilsner

This beer bombards the senses in an utterly wonderful way

Bready

P

Spicy

Floral

Woody

Pair this brew with any matter of cuisine or situation

From sushi to swiss cheese

Or from karate to knitting!

knitting myself a black belt

A three time gold medal award winning labor of love

2013   2014   2015

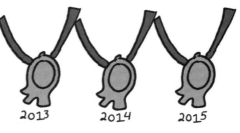

Great American Beer Festival gold medal for German Pilsner

BREWERY
Tröegs
Hershey, PA
NAME
Troegenator
STYLE
Doppelbock
ABV
8.2 %   German!

When the snow starts to fall...

I crave a doppelbock!

DOPPEL-
Double in German
BOCK- a stronger German Lager style

Lagers can take all colors and alcohol levels

They aren't just fizzy & yellow

Troegnator is warming, like a hug

oh my

BIG cherry notes

Stone fruit and woodsy flavors

In Germany, Bock beer is symbolized by the billy goat

guten tag

Bock beers came from Einbeck

Germany!

In North Central Germany

Said with a Bavarian accent- Einbeck sounds like Einbock

German for billy goat!

So cuddle up with the goat on a cold, winter day

* An 18th century slang term for old beer

And thus-
the IPA was born!

English style IPAs are
different than their
American cousin

They contain
British hops like
Fuggle

Known for
minty, floral
and earthy
tones

Mingled with toffee
tones from the malt

Yes sweetness is
okay in IPAs!

Bitter but thirst
quenching for
hot Indian
nights

And definitely British

Your
majesty-
more
beer?

Good Show!

And this came from
across the pond?!

Cool to see a
larger brewery
make a
beer
like
this

Great homage

Obviously pair with curry
and na'an

A cracking good
beer, by jove

Other British words

BREWERY
Alaskan
Juneau, Ak
NAME
Alaskan Stout
STYLE
Oatmeal Stout
ABV
6.2 %   British!

Despite its semi-remote location in Juneau, Ak...

...Alaskan Brewing is one of the BIGGEST breweries

Their year-round dark option is a classic Oatmeal Stout

Oatmeal has been used in beer for centuries

But when it was marketed for health...

For what ALES you!

...they aren't wrong!

Complex B vitamins

Antioxidants

Aids Digestion

Heart healthy

But you don't need health reasons to knock these back

Malty and smooth thanks to those oats!

OATS

True to style - a silky smooth, river of taste

Pair with hearty, bone-warming fare

or a beautiful Alaskan sunset in summer time

um- the sun doesn't set here

D'OH!

Boulevard Brewing is one of America's most respected breweries

Very True

What makes them stand out is a beer known as... Tank 7

Named for a temperamental tank at the facility

NO NO NO NO

Since farmhouse beers love to ferment at higher temps...

Tank 7 was the perfect place!

Some farmhouse ales have an aroma of light plastic

Like a tub full of grass clippings

that's a good thing!

These come from phenols- a by product of the yeast

A gift!

It's those phenols that give the beer its spicy flavor

Tank 7 is also bottle conditioned

whee!

whee!

whee!

Yeast are added to the bottle after packaging and then stored warm

This process gives the carbonation its BITE

And it also adds flavor!

One of the only American brewed Belgian style beers available in Belgium

Boulevard is also Belgian owned

And Belgians know quality

Pair with Belgian cuisine... frites!

BREWERY
Spencer
Spencer, MA
NAME
Spencer Trappist Ale
STYLE
Belgian Pale Ale
ABV
6.5 %   Belgian!

In rural Massachusetts sits the beautiful Abbey of St. Joseph

Inside a building in the rear of their acreage sits one of the most advanced breweries in America

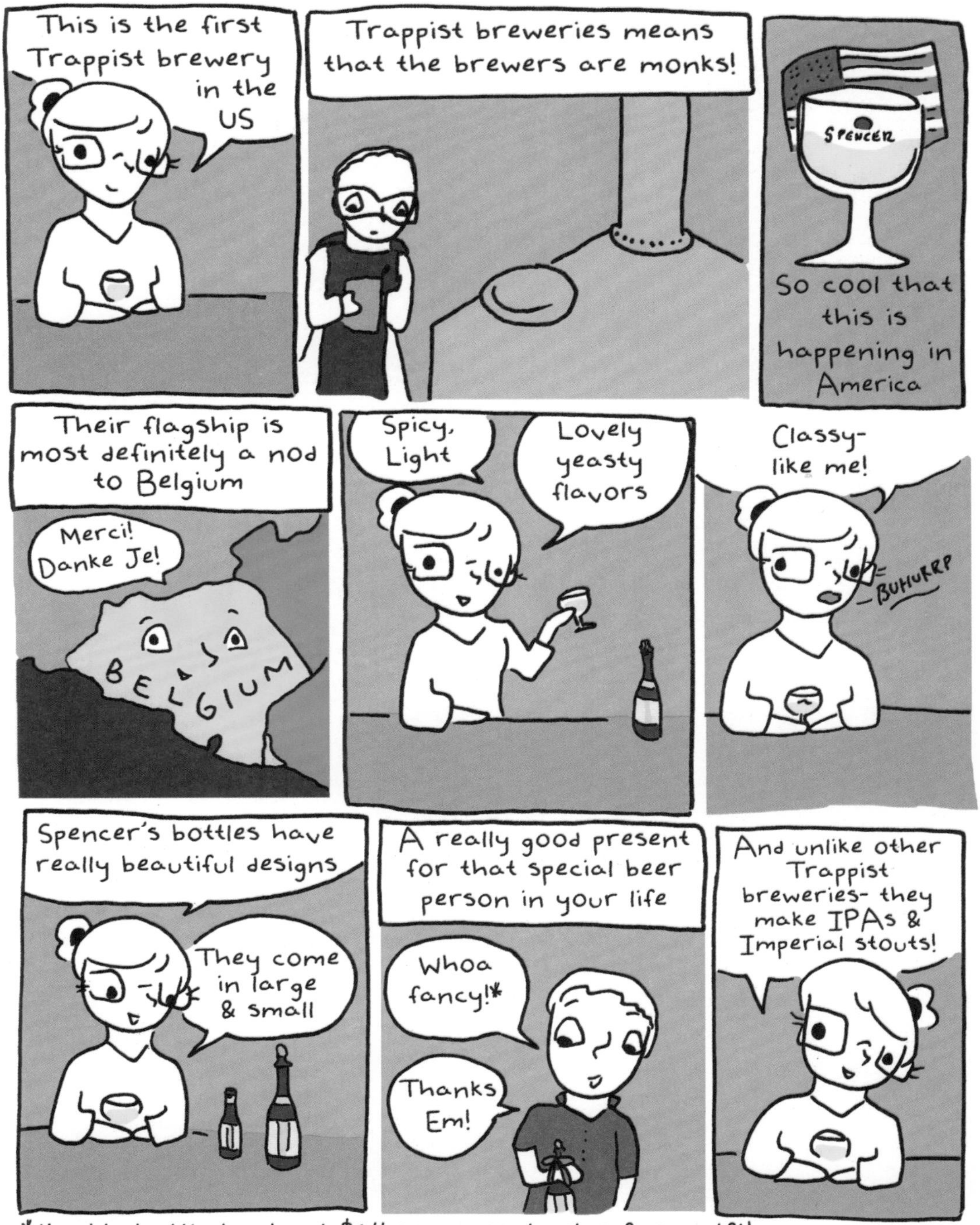
This is the first Trappist brewery in the US
Trappist breweries means that the brewers are monks!
SPENCER
So cool that this is happening in America
Their flagship is most definitely a nod to Belgium
Merci! Danke Je!
BELGIUM
Spicy, Light
Lovely yeasty flavors
Classy- like me!
BUHURRP
Spencer's bottles have really beautiful designs
They come in large & small
A really good present for that special beer person in your life
Whoa fancy!*
Thanks Em!
And unlike other Trappist breweries- they make IPAs & Imperial stouts!

*the big bottle is about $14 so a great price for a gift!

BREWERY
Lagunitas
Petaluma, CA
NAME
Pils
STYLE
Czech Pilsner
ABV
6 %

Czech Republic!

In 1842 - The city of Pilsen in what is now the Czech Republic, a beer was brewed that changed the world

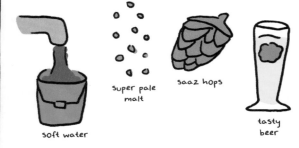

soft water

super pale malt

saaz hops

tasty beer

Not the first lager but a new style...
On a BIG scale

Czech Pils creator Josef Groll

Now many American breweries pay homage to this style

California brewing kingpin Lagunitas brews a fantastic pilsner

soft and pillowy

whack

True to style

A wonderful bready taste

Lagers LOOK simple

BUT NO WAY

They ferment twice as long as ales

48°F

with MUCH colder temperatures

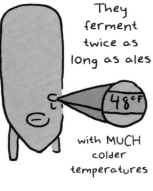

No room for error- right Brewmaster Jeremy?

Correct Em!

Lagunitas is known for mostly brewing hoppy beer

But they are more than just hops

Bring a six pack of pils and their IPA to please all palates

Great pils

Great IPA

BREWERY
Von Trapp
Stowe, VT
NAME & STYLE
Vienna Lager
ABV
5.2 %   Austria!

Sorry - Have to

The Hills are Alive...

With the sound of...beer!

The Von Trapp family owns a chalet hotel in the Green Mt of Vermont

The Trapps built a state of the art brewery down the road from their hotel...

wow!

Fancy German engineering!

so the youngest son of Maria Von Trapp could enjoy the beers of his homeland

Alps!

Their Vienna Lager is just lovely

lightly toasty

A perfect pairing with jam and bread

Or singing contests!

Me- a name I call myself

A little fruity

But fresh and approachable

Plus easy to drink!

A good crowd pleaser if you have a Von Trapp sized family!

Prost!

WOOD

Beer today ages mostly in steel

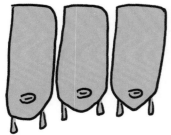

Breweries are full of these fermenters

But until recently – beer, like wine and liquor, was barrel-aged

Now barrels are used for speciality beers

The sky is the limit!

↑ Wine barrels

↑ Gin barrels

↗ Whiskey barrels

↑ Maple syrup barrels

↑ Scotch barrels

etc!

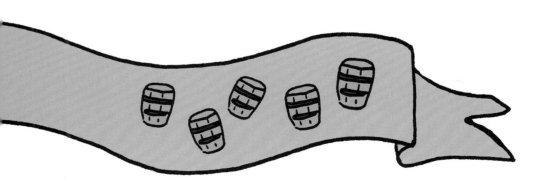

Breweries love "2nd run" barrels

So much possibility!

Breweries will use barrels that give their beers an added boast

They make beer more complex!

Breweries will also use fresh oak barrels too

Cocoa! Good call

COCOA POWDER

After all- beer can be a blank slate

Beer can age in the barrel for a few weeks...

...and some age for years!

Whoa!

1999

It's all at the discretion of the brewer

It's ready!

BREWERY
New Belgium
Ft. Collins, CO
NAME
La Folie
STYLE
Flanders Oud Bruin
ABV
7%

Oak Foeder!

Whoa

A foeder - pronounced "fooder" is a large oak vessel

for aging beers

A practice that's been used since the old days in Flanders

Not THAT Flanders

diddly!

New Belgium wanted to make sours like they do in Europe

Like Oud Bruins or Flanders Reds

So in the early 90's they brewed a beer called "La Folie"

French for "The Folly"

Americans were not digging sours back in those days

Now La Folie is a folly no more and is one of New Belgium's hottest beers!

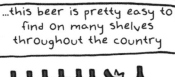
HUGE sour candy notes

Plus wood and cherry too

Reminiscent of a sour cocktail

Although this beer can take years to brew...

almost there

...this beer is pretty easy to find on many shelves throughout the country

Easy to find but super hard to forget....yum!

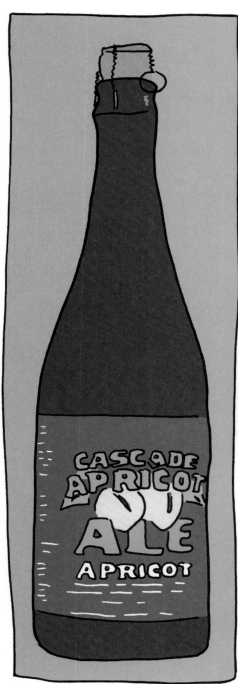

BREWERY
Cascade
Portland, OR
NAME
Apricot Ale
STYLE
American Wild Ale
ABV
8.5%
Oak Barrel!

Portland, Oregon-
Beer wonderland!

Beers are everywhere in PDX

Lagers, sours - all kinds!

Visit Portland and you'll find beer in bike shops & bakeries

One of the places to discover a crazy breed of beers is Cascade Brewing's Barrel House

Cascade has been making sour beers since 2008

My favorite is one of their originals

Apricot!

Aged in oak- the fruit flavor really shines!

But Beware...

They are not foolin' about the sour taste!

We're talking like the most sour candy you can think of!

For fans of sour who maybe aren't into beers yet...

I think you just found them their birthday present

Open it!

WHOA!

This is beer?!

Now try the cherry!

JACK'S ABBY
CRAFT LAGER

MOLE
BOURBON
BARREL-AGED

FRAMINGHAMMER

BALTIC PORTER

~/~

BREWERY
Jacks Abby
Framingham, MA
NAME
Mole Framinghammer
STYLE
Baltic Porter
ABV
12%
Bourbon Barrel!

Mole is a Latin American sauce

made with cocoa and spices!

It's also become a popular additive in beer!

Jack's Abby added mole

to their barrel-aged baltic porter

The baltic porter...

...plays well with the barrel, chocolate and chili flavor

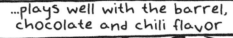

aces wild

dang!

A spicy, sweet mashup

A dessert in a glass!

Perfect after dinner

Very cool for a baltic porter to get this treatment

Especially from a brewery that mostly only does German lagers

Same for after a big meal

A great digestif!

Pair with a feast—chili, roast beef, heavy fare!

Age in the cellar or drink now

Share with friends!

The ABV is high octane

I remember when I first saw the Yeti

And I'm not talking about the mythic Nepalese creature

I'm talking about Great Divide's imp. stout

YUM

Great Divide has many yetis

original Oak espresso chocolate whiskey oatmeal

The chocolate version is barrel-aged with cocoa nibs and a dash of cayenne pepper!

This is best to drink at cellar temp.

55°

which is the ideal storing temp for beer!

Drinking it at 55 degrees allows for the flavors to come alive - cold beer masks taste!

Tastes like dark chocolate, subtle spices, and oak

To warm beer up, use your hands!

Enjoy after winter activities with new friends

Yeti! Wait up!

Guys, come on!

Make everyone try this beer- after all- CHOCOLATE!

BREWERY
Two Roads
Stratford, CT
NAME
Worker's Stomp
STYLE
Saison
ABV
7.5%

White Wine Barrel!

Full disclosure, Two Roads is my employer

And our beers are quite tasty!

YUM

One of the many reasons our brews are so tasty is our Master Brewer Phil Markowski. He's an author too!

Right on

farmhou ALES...

He ages a saison in wine barrels

white wine

HENCE THE NAME

This beer is important

because it showcases two things about beer

One- wine barrels add character and complexity to beer

And two- saisons in white wine barrels are made for each other

What a winery would consider trash...

Get Out Brett!

Brettanamyces

...a brewery would consider treasure

oh hey!

They add an amazing funky quality to beer

Big fruit

Spicy

Lovely wood notes

Splendid

Great for date night

Cheers to beer

Indeed!

Rare

Call me Ishmael– I mean...Em

As with anything– beers can be rare

Do I hear– $500?

In the beer world, they are called whales

BEER HO!

Because the hunt for them is epic

Almost any style can be a whale

And they are located all over the country

From many different breweries

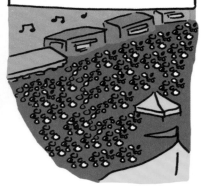

Some have parties around their releases like Cigar City in Florida

or acquire by waiting in line for hours or days

Only 12 hrs left

Or if you are really lucky

can you find it on the shelf

Be prepared to empty your wallet... they can be $$$

But however, once obtained...

YES!

where'd you get that?

Hahaha- from the HUNT!

...sharing them (or any beer really) is best with friends

If you are starting your whale spotting journey...

Founders Kentucky Breakfast Stout or KBS is one of the easier beers to spot with your spyglass

Kentucky Breakfast Stout is a bourbon barrel aged imperial oatmeal coffee stout

And we are talking big flavors here!

!!!

Like a boozy chocolate chip cookie

Like whiskey?

then buy this!

It has this aftertaste...oh you feel like you are melting

worth it

KBS is a snugly beer—warm and dear

FOUNDER
KBS

Also age beers like this

Big beers change over time

2010   2016

Wow, you've aged so well!

Save for snow days

heads up!

You're melting again

Don't care

135

BREWERY
Tree House
Monson, MA
NAME
Bear
STYLE
Brown Ale
ABV
6.4%

Rare!

Treehouse brews some of the most sought after beers in the U.S.

Treasures
Gold
Silver
Treehouse
Cans
Dia...

Only sold at their brewery in rural Massachusetts, the line to buy their beers can reach up to 400 people long!

Welcome to Connecticut

Their IPAs are most sought after

They make many IPAs

But their rarer offerings are beers like Bear Brown Ale

Tree House named a beer after me?!

Bear (the beer) is a rich and malty brew

Almost Porter-like

Has a house paint aroma and flavor

In a good way of course!

Perfect for that first frost

Also 100% bear approved!

Two Paws up!

A perfect complement to dessert

Baking is a perfect activity whilst waiting in line

So...tiny! Guess we can share?

BREWERY
3 Floyds
Munster, IN
NAME
Dark Lord
STYLE
2015 Russian Imperial Stout
ABV
15 %   Rare!

Most rare
beers tend
to be

Imperial
Stouts

Why?

Could be taste

Or high ABV

One of the hardest to procure
is only available on a single day
in Indiana

TOWN OF
MUNSTER

ENTER THE

DARK LORD

A 15% ABV (that's higher than wine!) imperial stout

Dark Lord?

Hello Friend!

This beer ages well. I had the 2015 vintage

wax indicates the year

Warming like a big coat

Beers like this have a viscosity that's similar to motor oil

that's a good thing!

It's as though it's not beer at all

more like a liquor

Flavors Include:

SMOKE

CHOCOLATE

STONE FRUIT

Who wants some beer!?

So who is this guy?

ME ME

Him?

He's my new friend!

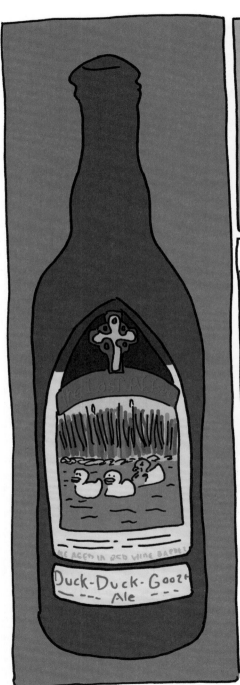

BREWERY
Lost Abbey
San Marcos, CA
NAME
Duck Duck Gooze
STYLE
Gueuze
ABV
7%

Rare!

Lost Abbey makes brilliant beers

Under the guidance of Tomme Arthur

Thx!

One of their beers makes a BIG splash in the beer world...

Gueuzes are made with yeast from the air

Lambic
Lambics are then aged and blended with other lambics to create gueuzes

The practice is pure Belgium

It takes time

Maybe that's why people seek them out

This beer is one of Lost Abbey's most sought after offerings

OMG

Maybe it's the unique flavor that people are drawn to

I mean unique!

Sort of like a tire

I mean that in a good way of course!

Sour too!

Always different

A wonderful celebration milestone beer

Lost Abbey also makes many other quacktastic offerings

BREWERY
Russian River
Santa Rosa, CA
NAME
Pliny the Younger
STYLE
Imperial IPA
ABV
10.25%   Rare!

Every February, a line forms around the Russian River Brewpub

RUSSIAN RIVER

To try an IPA dubbed

BEST IN THE WORLD!

or at least

the rarest

Younger is considered the 1st "Triple IPA"

The Biggest Hops!

More Booze! High ABV!

Each year the beer is different

azacca

comet

This year, it was brewed with azacca and comet hops

This year's was...

SO tropical!

It's Fermented colder, so the high ABV is very, very well hidden- wow!

and because every year is different...

...the beer evolves with the years

Plus it's what the owners of Russian River want to drink

A true labor of love

So wait in line- it's worth it! And when you do get the beer, pair with Russian River's pizza

YUM!

Taste

Let's talk about your mouth

The tongue and mouth

are full of thousands of taste buds

Working with the brain

and the nose

Flavor and taste are born!

mmmmmm...burger!

There are five flavors we as humans can taste

SWEET	SOUR

Malt forward beers like scotch ales or doppelbocks

Wild ales or Belgian lambics

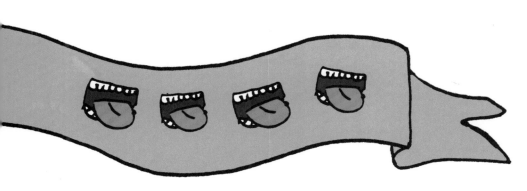

SALTY	BITTER	UMAMI or SAVORY

GOSE or Dortmunder Export

Pale Ales or India Pale Ales

Oyster stout

Beers can impart multiple tastes as well

 Goses are salty and sour

 Pale Ales can be bitter and sweet

By trying more beers responsibly, you can discover the tastes you are drawn to!

practice makes perfect

BREWERY
Abita
Abita Springs, LA
NAME
Strawgator
STYLE
Helles Bock
ABV
8 %
Sweet!

I love strawberries!

Fun to pick in the heat of the sun

Abita Brewing makes a killer strawberry lager in the summer

And they make Strawgator all year!

Remember that pink medicine you got as a kid?

BREWERY
Tallgrass
Manhattan, KS
NAME
8-bit
STYLE
American Pale Ale
ABV
5.2%   Bitter!

Tallgrass Brewing makes a year-round 8-bit pale ale

Yes, there will be a lot of video game jokes coming at you

It's one of their most popular beers, which makes sense since they are brewed in a college town...
GO WILDCATS!

KS

For a pale ale- it's surprisingly bitter!

46 IBUS

High for a pale

International Bitterness Units
-Measures bitterness in beer
-Number means how much of hop breakdown is in beer
Pale Ale 30-50 IBU
IPA 45-70 IBU

But bitterness can be very pleasant- like the rind of a grapefruit

With a color like the hair of Princess Toadstool

You think so?

It's sessionable, and in a cool can

Pack in your bag when you hit the forest with Link

We there yet?

No!

Or use it as the beer of choice for a marathon gaming session

I win again!

Great choice from the Heartland!

BREWERY
Wicked Weed
NAME
Medora
STYLE
American Wild Ale
ABV
6.6%
Sour!

Asheville, NC - one of the best beer cities

In one of the most beautiful places!

There are many breweries in town, but one of the best-known ones is Wicked Weed.

Hops are a wicked and pernicious weed

- Henry VIII

From IPAs to sours, they do it all

Wicked Weed consists of two breweries

FUNKATORIUM

This is their barrel age facility

When breweries talk funk, they don't mean funk music from the 70's

They mean wild yeast - like our buddy lactobacillus

Hey!

And when that lacto meets raspberry

It's love!

And the romance of fruit and yeast is just....

MAGICAL

If you like the natural tartness of fruit...

...then you'll love this

Perfect for a bucolic patio party overlooking the Great Smoky Mountains. Pair with creamy cheeses!

Sigh

BREWERY
Westbrook
Mt. Pleasant, SC
NAME AND STYLE
Gose
ABV
4 %

Salty!

When Westbrook Brewing opened...

...one of their beers shook up the scene

In America, the gose style is more sour

Moreso than its German cousin

People point to this beer as a new style- "Contemporary Gose"

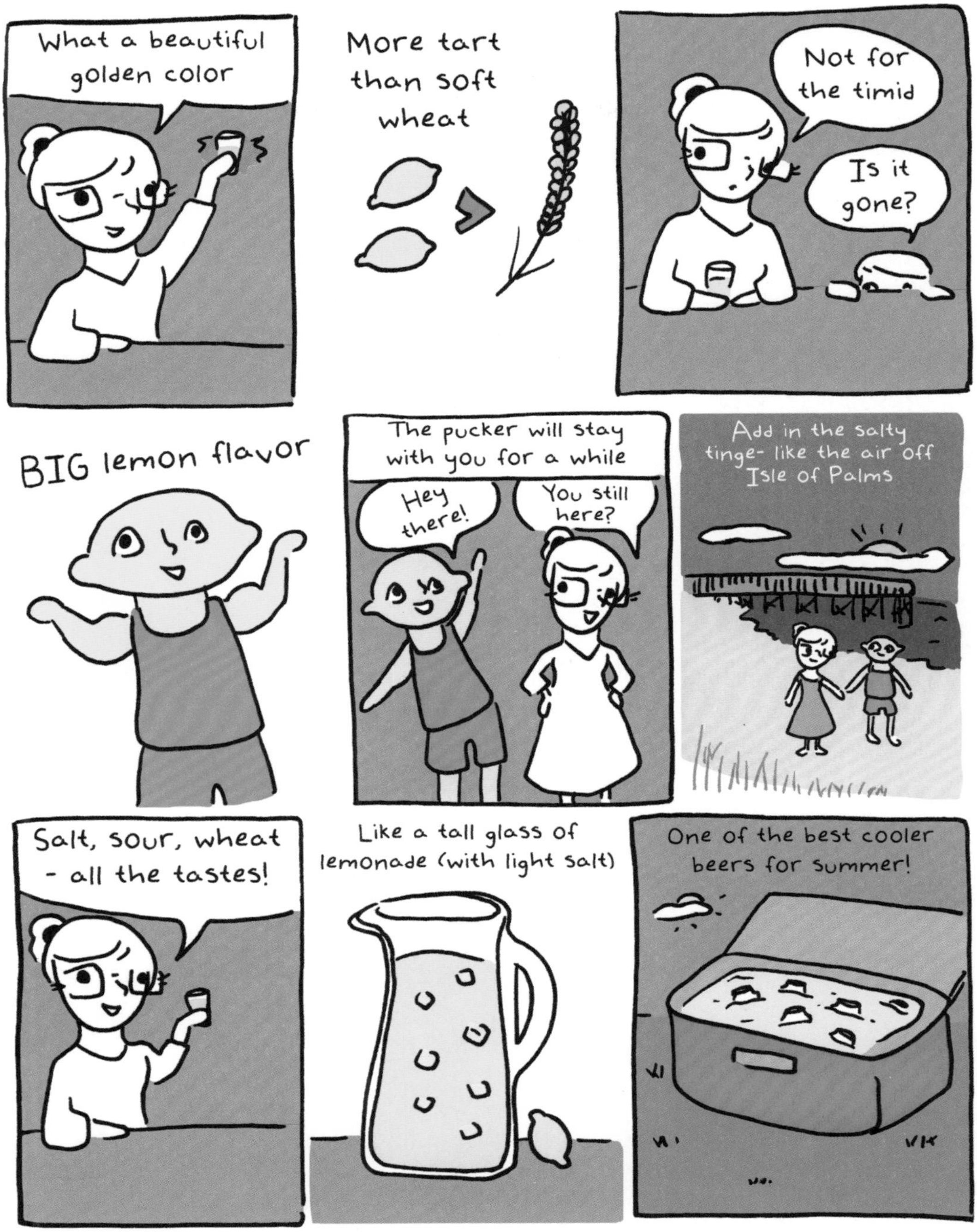
What a beautiful golden color
More tart than soft wheat
Not for the timid
Is it gone?
BIG lemon flavor
The pucker will stay with you for a while
Hey there!
You still here?
Add in the salty tinge- like the air off Isle of Palms
Salt, sour, wheat - all the tastes!
Like a tall glass of lemonade (with light salt)
One of the best cooler beers for summer!

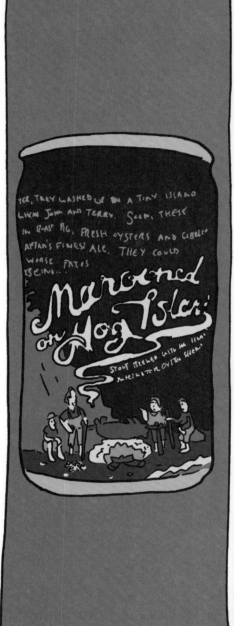

BREWERY
21st Amendment
San Leandro, CA
NAME
Marooned on Hog Island
STYLE
Oyster Stout
ABV
7.9 %

Umami!

Yes, you read that correctly

Oysters in a beer!

First appearing in 1920's London

Shells or whole oysters are added to the boil

21st Amendment teams up with a local oyster company for this beer

Hog River Oysters give their shells for use in the brew

In a good way!

The shells impart a chalky flavor to the beer

Good beer for bayside imbibing

Rich malt

Light brine

Silky

Higher ABV too

If oysters repulse you...don't worry

The beer isn't slimy like me!

Although try me again, I swear I'm delicious

If you DO like oysters, pair this beer with all kinds

From Blue Point to Wellfleet

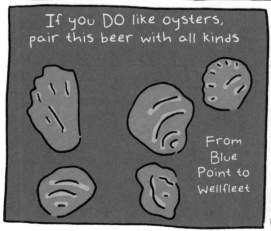

Stouts and oysters just go together

You said it missy!

Beer and Food

Now that we know flavor...

LET'S EAT

Breakfast

Lunch

Dinner

There's a beer for every meal

and I mean ANYTHING

Really!

Using the five tastes

SWEET
SALTY
BITTER
SOUR
UMAMI

Plus curiosity and a willingness to try new things

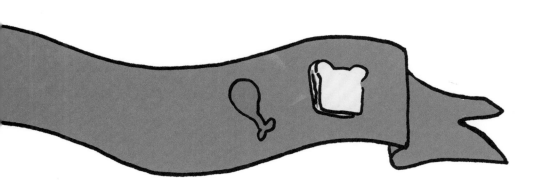

You can discover your favorite pairing

I love chili and black lagers

Some notable or odd food pairings

Dry Irish Stout

oysters

India Pale Ale

carrot cake

saison

brie

And with many different beers working for the same food...

Beer should definitely be invited to the table

LET'S DIG IN

Oatmeal isn't just for stouts

It's also used to haze up IPAs

Or used in traditional farmhouse ales

Since oatmeal is part of a balanced breakfast...

...what about an oatmeal porter?

I've seen a lot of oatmeal stouts

What's the difference?

STOUT vs. PORTER

Stouts use unmalted barley

Until recently a stout was just a strong porter

Porters are thinner in body and use malted barley

So a porter...

oh wow this is great

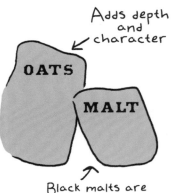

Adds depth and character

OATS

MALT

Black malts are reminiscent of coffee

Drink with a big breakfast

or lunch or dinner!

The kind of beer that'll give you confidence

BEER REALLY is for EVERYONE!

clap clap clap clap

clap clap clap clap clap

Or for low key Sundays with the crossword

What the heck is 12 down?

A malt drink? Four letters

Skip the overloaded bloody mary

Is that a burger?!

Beer CAN be for breakfast!

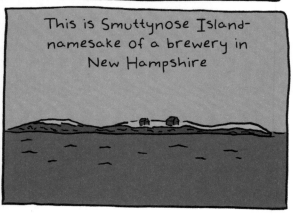

BREWERY
Smuttynose
Hampton, NH
NAME
Old Brown Dog
STYLE
Brown Ale
ABV
6.5 %
Lunch!

This is Smuttynose Island- namesake of a brewery in New Hampshire

Their beers are a staple of New England

One named after a certain senior canine

Despite the age- I can still fetch

Old Brown Dog was one of my first fav beers

Fruity, sweet...

...sort of reminds me of a sweet raisin loaf of bread

One of the beers that cemented my love of beer

approachable, tasty!

perfect for after office get togethers

It's as satisfying now as it was 10 years ago

A constant- one of those beers that's always there, always good

Brown ales are perfect

with a tasty ham sammy

or a gooey, chewy, ooey grilled cheese

Sit! Stay!

Good dog, Good beer!

BREWERY
Swamp Head
Gainesville, FL
NAME
Smoke Signal
STYLE
Smoked Beer
ABV
6.8 %   Dinner!

Florida is the land of sun, sand and...beer?

Florida's breweries make all manner of beers...including darker smoked beers

Back in the day, malt was kilned with wood!

So almost all beers made had smoky flavor

With the invention of coal fire kilns...

...beer lost its smoky taste

Swamphead's smoked beer

isn't like a campfire

And doesn't have any of the bacon flavor

of classic German smoked beers or "rauchbiers"

The smoky taste is there

But smooth

Balanced!

I'm not overwhelmed here

Smoked beers pair SO well with many foods

Best with brats!

Or better yet- cook with it!

Add to chili or stews

YUM!

Imparts that flavor to the foods

Or if you're in Florida- Grill up!

Great day for a beer!

BREWERY
Foothills
Winston-Salem, NC
NAME
Sexual Chocolate
STYLE
Russian Imperial Stout
ABV
9.6%   Dessert!

Yep, Sexual Chocoalte

The perfect beer to end on

One of the most sought after beers in the South

Sexual Chocolate is an imperial chocolate stout

And like the name implies...

...it's as silky smooth as an expensive dressing gown

with jazzy, big, bitter chocolate intensity

A good Valentine's Day beer

I love you!

Higher alcohol and warming

Not too boozy

Pair with dessert!

Like chocolate mousse or cake

The perfect nightcap

Should we retire?

oh yeah!

See?

Beer CAN be romantic

Who is Thomas Jefferson?

START YOUR BEER JOURNEY

Subscribe to magazines!

READ!

The Complete Beer Course — Josh Bernstein

Tasting Beer — Randy Mosher

The Beer Bible — Jeff Alworth

Great Beers of Belgium — Michael Jackson

Learn up on beer styles!

The Beer Judge Certification Program (BJCP) app is free — a listing of every beer style!

Visit local bars/breweries!

Most will let you taste and try before you buy

Just keep exploring!